# AUTOGRAPH
# LETTERS &
# MANUSCRIPTS

# AUTOGRAPH LETTERS & MANUSCRIPTS

## Major Acquisitions of

## The Pierpont Morgan Library

## 1924-1974

## NEW YORK

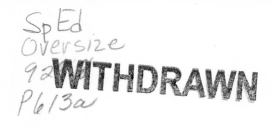

# CONTENTS

# PREFACE

THIS volume contains fifty examples of autographs, ranging from one of Pope Adrian IV in 1155 to that of John Steinbeck in 1961. They illustrate notable acquisitions in the Department of Autograph Manuscripts and Documents of The Pierpont Morgan Library during its fifty years as a public institution. The collections of this department include autographs in Western European and American literature since 1500 and in the other arts, historical manuscripts after the middle ages, and letters and documents of whatever period, save those on papyri or on clay tablets. The group of manuscripts of masterpieces of English literature is probably the finest in America, and the documents and letters of the Italian Renaissance and the musical autographs stand with the two or three most distinguished libraries in this country. Other periods of concentration are those of the Reformation in Germany, the Tudor and Stuart periods in England, and the American Revolution and early years of the republic.

The first autographs collected for what is now The Pierpont Morgan Library came as early as 1851, when Pierpont Morgan was only fourteen. In the next three or four decades the autograph collections grew slowly with a few very choice single letters and manuscripts purchased by him and by his father, Junius. After 1890, however, large groups were added which formed the basis of the principal periods and areas of concentration described above, except for music, which is largely a recent interest of the Library. Thousands of letters and documents of the nobility and royal houses of England and Europe, presidents, popes, bishops (especially of the Protestant Episcopal Church), and writers and artists of every rank, were bought, often in extensive series.

Two important guides to the autograph collection are those by Professor George K. Boyce, "Modern Literary Manuscripts in the Morgan Library," in *Publications of the Modern Language Association of America*, 1952, and Mr. Herbert T. F. Cahoon in the *Review of Acquisitions, 1949–1968*, published by the Library in 1969. Mr. Cahoon, who has been Curator of Autograph Manuscripts since 1954, has been responsible for this present publication; he has been helped, particularly with the musical autographs, by Mr. J. Rigbie Turner, and in certain translations by Mrs. Ruth Kraemer.

These two check-lists reveal above all our strength in English literary manuscripts. During the last fifty years we have continued to add more English autographs than American or Continental, and this continues to be true. Our collection of American literature and history is about half the size of the English manuscripts; the French, perhaps half that of the American autographs. In the past few decades many libraries in the United States have made American literature and history their primary concern, and we have therefore turned increasingly towards other areas where our national libraries were much weaker: to the Renaissance, and to highly significant letters and documents of Continental literature and history. We have also bought musical manuscripts and children's literature. Since the art collections of the Library are so important, we feel that is it especially valuable to have in the same building as the great cabinet of drawings the letters and papers of English and European artists. We have in recent years therefore added a considerable number of their manuscripts to the strong holdings of the Library. More and more in the Department of Autographs, as in the other main divisions of the Library, the accessions have been made, not in competition with other American libraries, but to guarantee a wider range of materials in America for the use of our own scholars and those throughout the world.

The fifty manuscripts illustrated here provide a fine sampling of scripts and styles of handwriting. They as well show the development and the breadth of an illustrious international collection of autographs.

Charles Ryskamp, *Director*

# INTRODUCTION

THE past fifty years have been of utmost significance in the development of the collection of autographs as well as of the other collections in The Pierpont Morgan Library. There have been major purchases as important material became available; many of the most valuable have been those made because of the generous gifts received from the Fellows of the Library.

The autograph collection may be said to have had its beginning as far back as 1851 when J. Pierpont Morgan, aged fourteen, wrote for and was sent the autograph of Millard Fillmore, in an envelope franked by the President himself. This was followed by a successful correspondence which brought the young man signatures of Protestant Episcopal bishops. As a consequence, autograph letters and documents of American presidents and bishops are strongly represented in the Library today. Pierpont's father, Junius, was also a collector and owned a superb six-page autograph letter of George Washington of 1788 expressing his hope for the new nation, as well as the original manuscript of Sir Walter Scott's *Guy Mannering*, the second of the Waverly Novels.

It was not until Junius Morgan's death in 1890 that Pierpont began to buy in earnest and on a magnificent scale. In the near quarter century, until his own death in 1913, he acquired many of the great manuscripts that appeared for sale, and, in his private library, laid the solid foundations of the Morgan Library. He was both aided and stimulated by his nephew, another Junius S. Morgan, who was a passionate connoisseur of books, prints, and manuscripts. A building for his private library was completed in 1906 and the brilliant young librarian, Miss Belle da Costa Greene, was employed to arrange and catalogue the collection and to help in its growth. These were the years during which the most notable manuscripts of Burns, Byron, Dickens, and Keats, among others, came to the Library; also the

Stephen H. Wakeman literary manuscripts of nineteenth-century America, including the Thoreau Journals.

J. P. Morgan, who inherited the Library from his father, took a keen personal interest in the collections and made many outstanding additions to them. Although he did not add to them in large numbers, he was especially attracted to the American historical albums brought together by his father: the autographs of the signers of the Declaration of Independence, the generals of the American Revolution, and the Articles of Confederation and the Constitution, and documents of the Siege of Yorktown. (J. P. Morgan presented a set of the signers of the Declaration of Independence to the Library of Congress, the first to be acquired by our national library, aside from the original document which was then in its custody.) Another favorite was the illustrated manuscript of Thackeray's *The Rose and the Ring*, which he acquired in 1915.

Both J. Pierpont Morgan and J. P. Morgan were generous in making items in the private library available to scholars, but there was a lack of working space and of a collection of reference books. No visitors were permitted in the Library when Mr. Morgan was away from New York. In 1924, believing that the Library had achieved too significant a position in our culture to remain in private hands, J. P. Morgan transferred it to a Board of Trustees with an endowment to provide for its maintenance. Soon afterwards it was incorporated by a special act of the legislature of New York State as a public reference library.

During the following decades, marked by financial depression and a second World War, the Library continued the gradual process of conversion from private collection to national asset. Scholars and visitors to the exhibitions came from all over the United States and Europe, and requests for information and for photographs and microfilms came and continue to come in ever increasing numbers.

The purpose of this present introduction is to give a brief summary of the fifty years that have gone by since the incorporation of the Library, insofar as they relate to autograph letters and manuscripts. The development of the collections has continued in the two best possible ways. One is the traditional Library policy of building "strength on strength"—our acquisitions of Dickens manuscripts are a good example of this. The other is the establishment of collections in important fields hitherto for the most part not associated with the Library; musical manuscripts and letters and manuscripts of contemporary authors illustrate this, the musical manuscripts most significantly.

Some fine manuscripts and letters were purchased by the Library in the 1920s and 1930s, and a few of them are illustrated here. There were letters of John Paul Jones, Martha and George Washington, Laurence Sterne, Lord Nelson, Carlyle, Sir Isaac Newton, Galileo, Tycho Brahe, Voltaire, Rousseau, and Robespierre, to name but a few. Gifts, except the many from J. P. Morgan, were minimal, mostly related to the history of the Morgan family, but both Presidents Theodore Roosevelt and Calvin Coolidge presented the manuscripts of their autobiographies—Roosevelt's in corrected typescript, Coolidge's in pencil autograph. Only a few manuscripts were acquired during the severest years of the depression, but these included Sir James M. Barrie's *Shall We Join the Ladies?*, Galsworthy's *The First and the Last*, and the "Codex Huygens"—the treatise on art history by the anonymous Milanese painter who was familiar with the notebooks of Leonardo da Vinci.

During the war years four manuscripts of first rank were purchased by the Library. They were Dickens' *Our Mutual Friend*, Swift's poem, "Apollo to the Dean," Elizabeth Barrett Browning's *Last Poems*, and Whitman's fair copy of his poem, "O Captain! My Captain!" In addition the Library acquired a number of fine autograph letters.

By 1950, money for purchases became gradually more plentiful and so did opportunities to spend it. At this time the Library also began to expand into new areas of interest. The continuing gifts of Mr. Reginald Allen's Gilbert and Sullivan collection started us on a musical road the length and breadth of which we did not then anticipate. Our Ruskin collection grew from a handful of autograph letters to a group of over 1600. These, with notable Ruskin manuscripts acquired early in the century, make us a center for Ruskin studies. Our good but slender Voltaire collection was increased by over 360 letters and much related material. Similarly our small Coleridge collection has had over 350 autograph letters added to it, so that it is now the largest single group in any institution. Our holdings of the letters of many other authors, especially English, were augmented on an extensive, nevertheless a more modest scale.

The Library's collection of autograph letters and documents of Renaissance figures became truly a major one with the purchase in 1950 of the Charles Fairfax Murray collection of 296 letters and related material dating from about 1400 to 1700. Nearly every letter is itself of real importance and a large number of the rulers, humanists, and artists of the Italian Renaissance are represented. Mrs. Harold T. White's recent gift of 420 letters dating also from the Italian Renaissance, plus a few later pieces, is a noteworthy addition and a fine source for scholars.

The collection of children's books presented by Miss Elizabeth Ball is one of the largest and most important of its kind. Although this is essentially a collection of books, it has been possible to add several manuscripts of books for children, including Richard Doyle's "Beauty and the Beast," and Saint-Exupéry's "Le Petit Prince."

In September 1968, the Cary Music Collection was deeded to the Library by the Trustees of the Mary Flagler Cary Charitable Trust. This collection of musical manuscripts and autograph letters of composers and musicians was the foremost private collection in this country. Through the interest and generosity of the Trustees we have been able to add many fine manuscripts and letters to it. Our holdings of French musical manuscripts have been greatly enriched and augmented by the gifts of Mr. Robert Owen Lehman. The leading French composers of the nineteenth century are now nearly all represented here, often by major compositions. These, with the deposits of The Heineman Collection and the private collection of Mr. Lehman, make the concentration of musical manuscripts under the roof of the Morgan Library one of two most important in the country.

As additions are made to the autograph collection each year, some pieces are examined by the conservation laboratory for paper repair or when authenticity is in question. As in many other libraries, bound volumes of letters or manuscripts are kept on shelves in our vaults, and individual or small groups of letters are kept in boxes in acid-free paper folders. The labelled folders are distributed in general classifications such as autographs by national origin: American, English, French, German, Italian; and by subjects: rulers of England, France, Spain, etc.; and artists, dramatists, and musicians.

Autograph manuscripts and letters are frequently shown in exhibitions for a variety of reasons: their intrinsic interest—sometimes sentimental—the excellence of the calligraphy, or, conversely, the changes and revisions made by the author. They are generally rare and unusual objects for the visitor to the Library, but their greatest value is to the scholar who works with them, deciphers them, and puts them into their historical and literary contexts. The Library is proud to have had so many of its manuscripts and letters used throughout the years—fifty and beyond—in the preparation of more perfect literary texts and more exact history.

Herbert Cahoon

# CATALOGUE

1

ADRIAN IV, POPE (D. 1159)

*Bull signed [Rome] 14 March 1155. 1 p. 77 x 60 cm.*

Nicholas Breakspear, the only Englishman ever to be chosen Pope, occupied the Throne of St. Peter from December 1154 to April 1159. In these few years he successfully guided the Papacy through a period of insecurity and many difficulties; he was even able to strengthen the power of the Papacy, especially in international affairs. When Henry II of England, however, desired to "extirpate the seeds of vice among the Irish people," Adrian made him a feudal grant of Ireland. The English suzerainty initiated by this Donation of Ireland continued for nearly eight centuries, and the name of Adrian is less revered by the Irish than by the English. This bull from the pontificate of Adrian IV is signed in full by him, "Ego Adrianus Catholicae Ecclesiae Episcopus," and by nine of his cardinals, including two future Popes, Alexander III and Lucius III. It is addressed to Rodulphus, Prior of the Benedictine monastery of the Camaldolites in the valley of Camaldoli, between Florence and Arezzo. It confirms the rule of the monastery over nearly fifty other monasteries and hermitages, and is an important document in the history of the Benedictine Order.

*Purchased as the gift of the Fellows, 1963.*

Ego Adrianus catholice ecclesie eps

Ego Adrianus [rota / papal monogram] BENE VALETE

Ego Iulius [...]

Ego [...] diac card [...]

LEONE BATTISTA ALBERTI, 1404–1472

*Autograph letter signed, Rome, 18 November* [1454] *to Matteo de' Pasti.*
*1 p. 19 x 21 cm.*

Alberti, one of the supremely versatile creators of the Italian Renaissance, achieved his greatest fame as an architect. His conversion of the church of San Francesco at Rimini into the Tempio Malatestiano is a subtle masterpiece of invention and adaptation. This letter is significant as the only surviving record by Alberti himself of his intentions regarding the final form of the classical marble shell to be erected around the original church; Pasti was apparently supervising the construction at the site. Alberti insists on the necessity of keeping inviolate the harmony of his façade, because "the least change distorts all the music." This letter was edited by Cecil Grayson and published with a facsimile by the Morgan Library in 1957 as *An Autograph Letter from Leon Battista Alberti to Matteo de' Pasti.*

*Purchased as the gift of the Fellows, 1956.*

Salve molto mi fu grato le lettere tue per più rispetti et fummi gratissimo el signior mio fa corto
chome io desiderava cioè che e' pigliassi optimo chonsiglio chon tutti. Ma quanto tu medesimo chol
manecto afferma chele chupole deno esser due larghezze alte. Jo credo più achi fece therme
et pantheon et tutte queste chose maxime che altri: et molto più alla ragio che apersone et
se lui sverggio a oppinione non mi maravgluero segli errera spesso. Quanto alfacto del pilastri
nel mio modello Ramentati chio tedissi questa faccia chonuien chesia opa dapse poche
queste larghezze et altezze delle chappelle mi perturbano Richordati e ponui mente che nel
modello sul chanto del tetto aman ritta et aman mancha ue una simile chosa. e dissi
questo pongho io qui pchoprire quella parte del tetto idest del chopto qual sifa
entro lachiesa poche questa larghezza dentro nossi puo moderare chonla nostra faccata
et uuolsi aiutare quel che fatto eno guastare quello che sabbia afare. Le misure et pporti
tioni depilastri tu uedi onde elle naschono: cioche tu muti si distorda tutta quella musica
et ragionamo dichoprire lachiesa di chosi leggiera. Nonui fidate sugwi pilastri adar
loro charicho. Et pquesto ciparea chella uolta inbotte facta di legniame fusse più utile.
hora quel nostri pilastro seno risponde legato chonquello della chappella non monta po
che quello della chappella noñ hara busognio daiuto et se lanostra facciata et se bene glibisogna
ello è stucino et quasi legato che lara molto aiuto. Adonque se chosi paltro ueparra seghuitu
el disegnio quale amio iudicio sta bene. Delfacto delli occhi. uorrei chi fa pfessione
intendessi el mestier suo. Dichami poche si squarca elmuro et indebolescono loedificio in
far fenestre. Pncessita dellume. Stumi puoi chomon indebolire hauere più lume non
fussi tu potessime farmi quel incomodo: Da man dricta aman mancha delloccio rima squar
ciato et tanto archo quanto et semicircolo sostiene elpeso dispra. disopra sta nulla più
forte et lauoro psspocio et è obturato quello che debba darui ellume però molte ra
gioni aquesto pposito. ma sola questa mi basti. che mai in edeficio lodato prsse achi intende
quello che niuno intende oggi. mai. mai uederai factou occhio sено alle chupole in luo
 gho della cherecha et questo sifa arerchotempij. a love a phebo. quali sono patroni della
luce et hano tanta ragione in la sua larghezza Questo dissi pmostrarui onde escha
el uero. Sequi uerra psona quanto sara inme daro ogni modo di satisfare al sigr mio
Tu pprori examina et odi molti et reficiscimi. forse qualchessia dira chosa da stimarla
Raccomandami Aulouro ostriui alsigr achui desidero miqualunque modo esr grato. Racc
al magn Rus et amouisg ecptho et atutti quelli achi tuesr cheme amino Se haro
fidato uimandero echaromphilo et altre Vale Roma xvij 458 Baptista Alb

3

FRANCISCUS PHILELPHUS, 1398–1481

*Autograph letter signed, Milan, 1478, to Ludovico Maria Sforza (Il Moro),*
*Duke of Milan. 1 p. with address. 25 x 18.5 cm.*

The noted humanist writes to his patron asking him to continue his benefactions, and adding that he is expecting more important news on various matters. He also gives news of the Trotti Bentivoglio family; they are intimate friends of the Sforzas and send greetings. This letter is from the large collection of Italian Renaissance autograph letters and documents, with some later additions, which were the gift of Mrs. White. The items, over four hundred in number, greatly strengthen the Library's holdings in an already strong field.

*Gift of Mrs. Harold T. White, 1969.*

4

NICCOLÒ MACHIAVELLI, 1469–1527

*Autograph letter signed [Florence] 5 June 1499, to Pietro Francesco Tosinghi.*
*1 p. 27 x 19.5 cm.*

An official communication to Tosinghi, who was Florentine Commissario generale of the forces against Pisa, reporting on the negotiations between Florence and the Duke of Milan for aid against Pisa, and giving news of the presence of Turks in Sicilian waters. From 1498 to 1512, Machiavelli served as Secretary of the Second Chancery of the Florentine Republic. This is one of three autograph letters of Machiavelli acquired with the Fairfax Murray Collection of European Autographs—a group of nearly three hundred important letters, mostly from the period of the Italian Renaissance.

*Purchased in 1950.*

ag.co vir. z.os. Hiui di fa el duca dimilano scripse ad qsto s. Et uolena che no anda
re piu aluno co noi z po si uolena obbligare z e suoi mi obbligassi z richiederaui
z omni uolta che li hauessi bisogno delli aiuti uostri noi fussi tenuti ad suirlo di 300
ho dar z 2000 fanti z che noi dnadassi qllo uoleui dalui p la recuparatione dipisa
rispossi a li nostri signori dopo qualche co sulta z omni uolta che lui defacto ce signorissi
liberamente dipisa z noi mi obbligaresti ad quato addimadaua: ma sendo la cosa
dormire z qsto ne portua seguire si giudicaua p icoloso oldeclararsi rispedo alla
cosa fromzese z sanza utilita disua s. z po si mouerua p lui ritrouare u
modo che sua ex.tia si assicurassi che uno si mouesse p iculo lostrato nostro: laquale
risposta no satisfa puno alla ex.tia diqllo s. z rispose ad li nostri on
rutto alterato: Et p qsta cagione a nostri signori e parso madaure uno
proprio adsua ex.tia p porlo meglio iustificarsi apsso di sua ex.tia z mostrarli
l amo da collo z li altro renocare da siena il quale ex.tia piu post domane
Questo e quato occorre hora diportanza: z ciascho di loro se ritrouare
co messua dalnero z oppinione z di qualcuno che si uadi alla uolta disicilia
p uero che z li ha facto oltro sforzo p rena z p mare che ciascuno sta
sospeso la: Et el duca dimilano anchora teme piu oltato della cosa dalnero
di fiancia z p essere piu tempo no ci es uenuto lettere ... tia si dubita
che el duca dimilano no le habbi iterceptate: a

S. io nelui ho scripto dialtrimo come io haueri desiderare ... cagione
la occupatione z anchora no ci essere uenuti aduisi se no ordinarij altro
n. no occorre se no racomadarmi alla s.io. vra: a xxviij z. 99 iiij

Nicholaus machiavellus

5

DESIDERIUS ERASMUS, 1467–1536

*Autograph letter signed, Freiburg, 30 August 1534, to Guy Morillon, secretary to the Emperor Charles V. 1 p. with address. 33 x 21 cm.*

This letter, written towards the close of the life of the great humanist, is dated from Freiburg, where Erasmus had at his disposal a house originally built for the Emperor Maximilian. Erasmus warns of the dangers of spreading sectarianism, and is grateful for the efforts towards peace being made by the Emperor. He concludes with a sad comment on intellectual liberty in England where the three most learned men are in prison: the Bishop of Rochester, the Bishop of London, and "—than whom I have never had a better friend—Thomas More."

*Purchased as the gift of the Fellows with the special assistance of Mrs. Landon K. Thorne and Mr. Alfred Ogden, 1955.*

S. P. ... te tantu[m] amicu[m] habeam ... Hispanis, miror iam annis aliquot me nullas accepisse litteras quid isthic agatur. Si quid Caesares agant nosse cupis, mihi qu...

De valetudine sua.

...

Pax in Germania.

... bonus Caesares ... quod pace[m] habet germania, qui maluit parem iniqua[m] q[uam] bellum aequu[m]. ...

Sette
Anabaptiste.

... negotium adhuc ... Anabaptiste no[n] alibi ... germaniam ... q[uam] olim ... Aegypt[ii]... homines lymphati ... morte donati. ... sed ... erit publicum latrocinium ...

Negotium cum Barbirio.

... Barbirius ... plane ... Hactenus ... coloribus ... tamen professus se velle solvere, proximis litteris scribit sedasse q[uod] ... non posse amplius. Suspicor illum suo commodo ...

De quibusdam viris doctis carceri mancipatis.

Vives scribit Ioan... ... in fratres Tobare ... alijs nonnullis bene doctis esse in carcere.
Scribo ... tres viros totius Angliae doctissimos ... in carcere, ... Ro[ffen]sem, ... Lo[n]doniensem ..., qua nihil ... habet amicius, Thoma[m] Morum.
Bene vale. Datum Friburgi Brisgoie 3. Cal. Sept. 1534

Erasmus Roterodamus manu ...

6

GIORGIO VASARI, 1511–1574

*Autograph letter signed, Florence, 4 January [1588] to Cosimo I de' Medici, Grand Duke of Tuscany. 1 p. 29.5 x 21.5 cm.*

The great Italian painter and art historian writes to his patron concerning designs for his paintings in the Palazzo Vecchio. This is one of about eighty letters of Vasari in the Library's collections and was acquired with the Fairfax Murray Collection of European Autographs.

*Purchased in 1950.*

Ill.mo et Eccell.mo S.r mio

Riceuej i Rescritti et V.E.I. a farsj nella mia lettera et aruto daro essito
secondo la Commessione di quella; sol resta et il vescouo di Cortona si ricorda
dello spedalito di Marsilia quanto il Caualje'r Rosso: inpero suplischa in
Canbio suo Mon S de Tornabuonj: et cio sia prima et puo: la lor' Cose saro
darne: Lo spedalingho de Nocentj mia daro la inclusa et Caldamiennt me la
raccomandara dessiderando et circha le Cose dello spedale quella sappia et
veglia lej et sara Contento per et incassi di quel Gouerno, no uol fare senza quel
et uole V.E.I. alla quale continuo meli raccomando: Io ho finito di
far Trascriuere il Dialogho delle stanze di sopra il quale lo Condoro Cosi
abozzaro si puo dire acagione et V.E possa secondo il suo Giudjto leuarne
et aggiugniere: Se V.E uole et Jo lo mandj aquella incanto et Jo distendo
questo delle stanze di sotto un Cenno basti: il Giudj na uisto potre q' basti
Dj Fiorenza allj iiij di Gennaio M D L VIJ

D V E Ill.mo

V.tt.mo S.
Giorgio Vasari

## TREATISE ON ART THEORY. ITALIAN (MILANESE). XVI CENTURY

*"Geometrical Scheme of Movements of the Body." [c.1560–80]. 128 leaves (folio 28 is reproduced here). 18.5 x 15.5 cm.*

This "Codex Huygens" takes its name from its seventeenth-century Dutch owner, the accomplished Constantijn Huygens, who for more than sixty years served the House of Orange, including William III of England. Huygens believed that these drawings by an anonymous Milanese artist were the work of Leonardo da Vinci, and remarked that he would not part with the Codex for four times the three and a half guineas it cost him. The 128 surviving pages of this projected "Regole del disegno" deal with the structure and proportions of the male and female figure, a theory of human movement, the proportions of the horse, perspective, and a theory of light and shade. The anonymous artist must certainly have been familiar with Leonardo's drawings. The Codex was edited by Erwin Panofsky and published, with a complete facsimile, by the Warburg Institute, London, in 1940.

*Purchased in 1938.*

28.

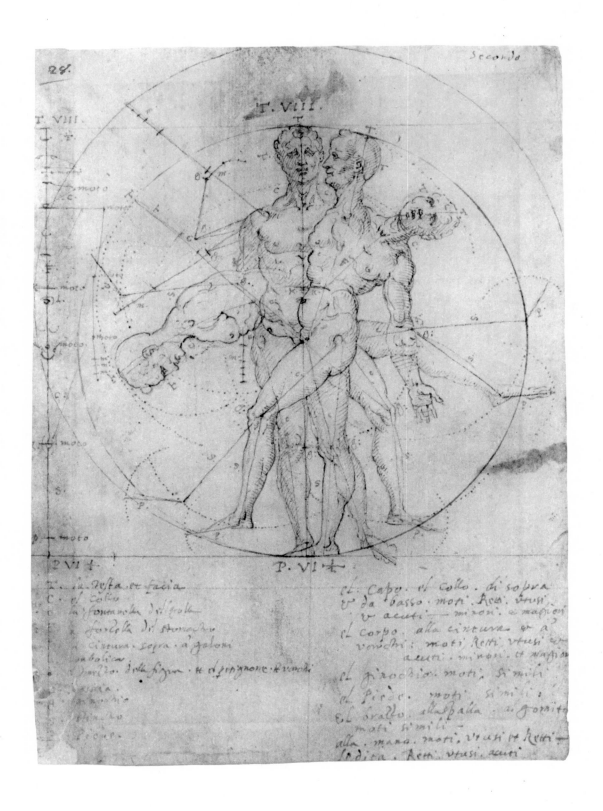

**8**

SIR PHILIP SIDNEY, 1554–1586

*"Defence of the Earl of Leicester." Autograph manuscript unsigned. [n.p., 1584].*
*14 p. 30.5 x 21.5 cm.*

One of the few surviving examples of an autograph manuscript by a leading Elizabethan author. Sidney vigorously defends his uncle, Robert Dudley, Earl of Leicester, against charges put forth in an anonymous pamphlet, *Leicester's Commonwealth*, by "a shameless libeller." At the end of the tract Sidney challenges the anonymous writer to defend his allegations with the sword. Sidney apparently wrote with a view to publication but this work remained in manuscript and was not printed until 1746. The "Defence" was acquired bound up with sixteen documents concerning various members of the Sidney family.

*Purchased with the assistance of the Fellows, 1953.*

## 9

FRANCIS BACON, VISCOUNT ST. ALBANS, 1561–1626

*Autograph letter signed, Windsor, 16 September 1604, to his brother, Sir Nicholas Bacon. 1 p. with address. 30.5 x 23 cm.*

While in the service of James I, Bacon informs his brother of the King's bestowal of the property of Dudley Fortescue, a suicide, on Thomas Buchanan and his wife. He asks the aid and favor of Nicholas when Buchanan comes to see the goods and chattels. At the lower left Bacon adds, "Excuse me I pray you; paper was short at this tyme." This letter is part of an important collection of letters, documents, and printed books by or relating to Francis Bacon brought together by Mr. Redmond and presented to the Library.

*Gift of Mr. Roland L. Redmond, 1946.*

Brother Baron Whereas it hath pleased the K. to
bestow vpon Mr Dr Burgonname and his wife beinge
of the Queenes Bedchamber, the leases, goods and
chattells of one Dudly Fortescue who latly
became felo de se, for as much as since the
sending of the Councell letters, it hath seemed
good to goe down himself about the busines he
being intreated by my ... good frend to commend
this busines to yor ayde and favour I doe
heartely desire you to further him what you may
I comend ... you it will be very well
taken at yor hands, and specially the K. will
thanke you for it, as a pleasure to a person
whom he doth extraordinarily affect. So
I comend you to Godds goodnes and
remayne

Excuse me I pray
you, paper was
not at hand
                                        Loving Brother
                                            and frend

                                        Fr Bacon

Court at Wyndsore
this 16th of Sept
1604

## 10

ESTHER INGLIS, 1571–1624

*Calligraphic manuscript. London. 1606. 33 leaves. 9.5 x 13.5 cm.*

This little manuscript, two pages of which are reproduced here, was executed for Master Thomas Puckering who, between 1605 and 1610, was a companion of Henry, Prince of Wales. It was presented to him on New Year's Day 1607. The text is written in various types of roman and italic scripts as they were known and practiced in Elizabethan and Jacobean England, with decorative borders, flowers, and birds in gold and colors. Miss Inglis was important both as calligrapher and teacher. The Library has a fine representative collection of later calligraphic works including some by Edward Johnston.

*Purchased as the gift of the Fellows, 1961.*

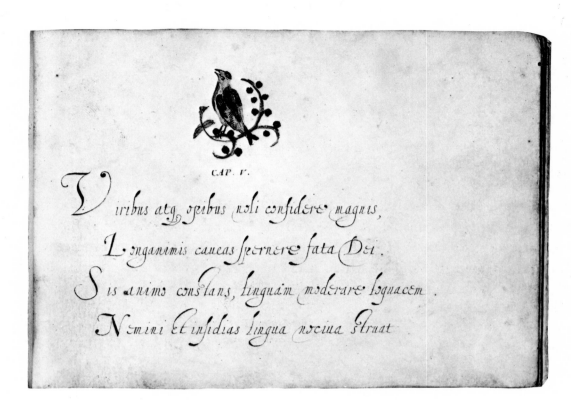

CAP. V.

Viribus atq̃ opibus noli confidere magnis,

Longanimis caueas spernere fata Dei.

Sis animo constans, linguam moderare loquacem.

Nemini et insidias lingua nociua struat

CAP. XXV.

Quæ sint pulchra docet, quæ sint inhonesta, beati
Qui nam sint vere disserit inde simul.
Multa nocent homini, sed cunctis foemina pejor,
Quæ proprio non vult rite subesse viro.

## 11

GUIDO RENI, 1575–1642

*Autograph account book of his work as a painter. [Rome] 1609–1612. 33 p.*
*13 x 10 cm.*

The account book covers the period from 25 October 1609 to 1 May 1612. These are years of great significance in the artist's career, the years of his service to the Cardinal Borghese and to Pope Paul V. At the outset of the period Reni is a promising talent among the younger Bolognese artists, but by the end of this period he is the leading artist of Rome. The account book was edited by D. Stephen Pepper and published in the *Burlington Magazine* in 1971.

*Gift of Mr. Robert H. Taylor, 1969.*

Adi 25 9mbre 1609

Dal Car.le Borghese per le
à buon conto à
Pitture fatte à questo giorno ho
ricevuto scudi ————————— 300

Adi 7 Novembre 1609                    6

Dal Car.le Borghese ricevuto
p resto delle Pitture di S. Greg.o
et il S. Pietro et S. Paolo à S. Maria
et questo p restante et saldo
quattrocento.

                    Adi 2 [...] 9mbre 1609
Cento scudi à Bon conto delle
Pitture che si faran nella Cap.lla
nova di Monte Cavallo.

12

WILLIAM HOLGATE, C.1590–1634

*"The Common-place Book of Mr. W. H." A collection of copies of contemporary (and occasionally original) poems of the seventeenth century. [c.1634?] 19.5 x 14.5 cm.*

A number of the poems in this most important collection have not been identified, but others are by Beaumont, Donne, Herbert, Ben Jonson, and Shakespeare. Reproduced here are Donne's "Song," and Shakespeare's sonnet no. 106.

*Gift of Mr. J. P. Morgan, 1927.*

**Dr. D:**

Go and catch a falling star,
Get with child a mandrake root,
Tell me where all past years are,
Or who cleft the Devil's foot,
Teach me to hear mermaids singing,
Or to keep off envy's stinging,
  And find
  What wind
Serves an honest mind.

If thou be'st born to strange sights,
Things invisible to see,
Ride ten thousand days and nights,
Till age snow white hairs on thee,
Thou, when thou return'st, wilt tell me
All strange wonders that befell thee,
  And swear
  No where
Lives a woman true, and fair.

If thou find'st one, let me know,
Such a pilgrimage were sweet;
Yet do not, I would not go,
Though at next door we might meet;
Though she were true, when you met her,
And last, till you send your letter,
  Yet she
  Will be
False, ere I come, to two, or three.

  Finis

---

**Dr. D.**

When my heart was mine own, and not by vows
By thee o'red, nor by my lights breathed into thee
What looks what flames, what perfumes what shows
Did humbly begg and steal my heart from me,
Through times eyes, mine thought I might behould
Thy heart as pictures through a crystal sigh
Thy heart seems soft, and pure as liquid gould
Thy faith firm bright and durable as brass
But as all promise so they have obtains
First sovereignty to guild their words and deeds
With ... and right which thy have stayed
Full sway done lastly thin show victorious deeds
So after conquest thou dost miss my sect
Could not (thy once pure) heart off now forbear
May move above an amorous respect
To any other? Oh towards me I frown
Thy heart to break, that faith to wax both treym
Which takeings breath from sun's amorous eye
Melts with thin flames at once more, and burns.

---

And on each side two fair limbs for defence
(As keepers fit for beauty's excellence)
Stand, and from thence, two slender twigs take life,
Mutually managing with out any strife,
And are the founders of this goodly frame
Least to of mortals his fate should form lame,
In his unbowelled bosom, thought it meet,
To furnish all with two most pretty feet.
But what have I forgot? Where had I three now?
Forgive, but they were wont most to my mind,
Fairer I not reckon I should them forget
That man intend me, therefore near in their debts,
Yet each, me shew Here is a way to enter
Into rich boyes, fish on then thighs venture.
These little doves, in fashion like two shells
Of mother of pearl, strange seemly still,
That though Meander-like the tide go it,
The sweet shall find an easy way to hit,
And that same house which him thinks secure,
Shall bring him out again, with out a showr,
But of I never saint, tell me but enter yet
And lock me even in the cabinet
So thy sweet memoir where let me dwell
See I make my prison secure, and freedom's Hell.   Finis

---

**On his Mistress Beauty**

When on the Annals of all wasting time
I see description of the fairest wight
And beauty making beautiful old mind,      anne
Then on the blazon of sweet beauty's knights
In praise of ladies dead and lovely knights
Then on the blazon of sweet beauty's best
Of face of hand, of lip, of eye, or brow
I see their antique pen would have exprest
Even such a beauty as you master now
So all these praises were but prophecies
Of this our time, all you prefiguring
And for they saw but with divining eyes
They had not skill enough your worth to sing
For we, which now behold these present days
Have eyes to wonder, but no tongues to praise.   Finis

## 13

LOUIS XIV, KING OF FRANCE, 1638–1715

*Autograph letter signed, Paris, 9 September 1651, to Cardinal Mazarin.*
*22.5 x 17 cm.*

This letter, entirely in the young King's hand, is one of great historical significance. Two days before it was written, the King, aged thirteen, declared his majority in the Parlement of Paris. Several years before this date the Cardinal had managed to incur the hatred of many Frenchmen, bourgeois and nobles alike, except for his own powerful group of personal followers. The opposing forces closed in on him and he was forced into nearly a year of exile. Here the King asks him to return to his service as soon as he can travel with safety. He promises that his return will obliterate in the most official manner all the injustices Mazarin has suffered during the King's minority. This is a significant addition to the Library's large collection of autographs and documents of European rulers and their courts.

*Gift of Miss Julia P. Wightman, 1970.*

~~[crossed out]~~ qui fust arrachée a la Reyne
madame ma mere par la violence des
ennemis de mon estat et les vostre qui
ne luy laisserent ni la liberté ni la pui
ssance de la refuser et comme elle est
pleine d'outrage d'accusations et de calom
nies mon honneur et ma conscience
mesme m'obligent d'authoriser vostre
innocence dans tout mon Royaume et de
faire connaistre a tous mes subjets les
satisfactions et les avantages qui me
demeure de vostre capasité et fidelité
dans l'administration que vous eus de mon
estat que la sagesse et vos conseils m'aurroi
rendu plus pesible et le plus glorieus
du monde si les diverses factions qui se
sont formées et les puissance qui les ont
sout enus vous en eusent laisé la conduite
libre, je finiray en vous asseurant que je suis
vostre bien bon et affectioné cousin

a paris ce 8e 2                            LOUIS.
septembre 1651.

14

JEAN BAPTISTE RACINE, 1639–1699

*Autograph letter signed, Paris, 1661, to his sister, Marie, in their home town of La Ferté-Milon near Soissons. 3 p. with address. 16.6 x 11 cm.*

Racine chides his sister for not having written to him in Paris and concludes that she must be annoyed with him; he will do everything to make amends. He gives news of the family and asks for her confidence in him. Although the letter itself is undated, the date accepted by scholars is 1661, when the great dramatist was twenty-two years of age; only eleven earlier letters from him are known. This is the first Racine letter to come to the Library, where it joins a fine collection of his first editions.

*Purchased as the gift of the Heineman Foundation, 1965.*

Ma très chère sœur

J'ay manqué jusques icy l'occasion pour vous écrire. En voicy Dieu mercy une assez belle, par le moyen de mon Cousin du Chesne qui s'en va. Je ne manqueray pas une de toutes celles qui se présenteront. Mon Cousin Vitart doit aller encore bientost à la Ferté, je luy donneray aussi une lettre. Plust à Dieu que vous fussiez dans la mesme disposition que moy, et que vous me voulussiez écrire quand vous pourriez. Mais au moins voit bien que vous manque plus de bonne volonté que d'autre chose. Car je vous ay déjà mandé mon adresse. Si je me m'en souviens, et il m'est aisé de me faire tenir vos lettres. Au moins j'en espérois que de vous tous les mois. Mais je voy bien que vous estes toujours en colère et que vous me voulez punir de ce que je n'ay pas esté ce vous semble assez diligent pour vous voir, tandis que j'estois à la Ferté. Je ny vous plus retourner de ma vie. Car je n'y ay pas fait encore un voyage qui ne m'ait mis mal avec vous. Et en cela je suis le plus malheureux du monde, puisque c'estoit plus pour vous que j'y allois que pour quelque chose que ce fust.

Je ne feray pas cette lettre plus longue, afin de garder de quoy en faire bientost une autre Mais au nom de Dieu écrivez moy, et adressez votre lettre à moy mesme, à l'image S. Louis près des Genevièves. Je vous le dis encore, afin que vous n'ayez point d'excuse. Je vous promets une entière exactitude de mon costé. Adieu je vous donne le bonsoir. Je puis bien vous le donner, car j'entends minuit qui sonne. Adieu donc ma chère sœur, et pardonnez moy toutes mes négligences, vous assurant que je vous seray à vous toute ma vie.

Racine.

Je vous manderay tout ce que je feray. N'écrivez rien de moy que je ne vous le mande.

## 15

JOHN LOCKE, 1632–1704

*"An Essay concerning humane understanding, in fower books." Manuscript of Books I and II. 383 p. 1685. 16.5 x 11 cm.*

After writing drafts of his *Essay* in 1671, other matters engaged Locke's attention. He was, however, able to make periodic revisions of it before its publication in 1690 and this revision of 1685 is the only one known to have survived. It is in a hand very much like that of Locke but one which is possibly that of a copyist; the corrections are certainly in Locke's hand. In any case, this is an important manuscript of a great philosophical work; it was first edited and published in its entirety in 1955.

*Purchased in 1924.*

An Essay concerning
Humane Understanding

Lib: 1. Cap: 1

1. Since it is ye understanding yt sets man above ye rest of sensible beings & gives him all ye advantage & dominion wch he has over y, it certainly is a subject ...

L.2.c.1
Of the Originall of our Ideas

1. Every man being conscious to himselfe yt he thinkes ...

**16**

CHARLES PERRAULT, 1628–1703

*"Contes de ma Mere L Oye." Manuscript in a scribal hand, dated MDCXCV, containing the dedicatory epistle to Mademoiselle Elisabeth Charlotte d'Orléans and five tales, decorated with seven gouache illustrations. 59 leaves. 19 x 13 cm.*

Until this volume was offered to the Library, it was not known that any manuscript survived of this cornerstone of all children's literature. It contains the tales known in English as "Sleeping Beauty," "Little Red Riding Hood," "Bluebeard," "Puss in Boots," and "Diamonds and Toads." In 1697, two years after the completion of the manuscript, they were published in a collection entitled *Histoires ou Contes du temps passé*, to which were added three more Perrault tales, among them, "Cinderella." The authorship of the tales has been attributed both to Charles Perrault and to his son, Pierre Perrault Darmancour. This manuscript was originally made for presentation to Mademoiselle, the spirited young niece of King Louis XIV. In 1956, the Morgan Library published a critical edition edited by Jacques Barchilon in which the manuscript is reproduced in full facsimile.

*Purchased as the gift of the Fellows, 1953.*

## 17

FRANÇOIS MARIE AROUET DE VOLTAIRE, 1694–1778

*Autograph letter signed, Chatenay, 12 June [1718], to the Earl of Ashburnham.*
*1 p. 19 x 13.5 cm.*

The letter asks for the loan of a horse, and the signature is "Arouet de Voltaire," the first surviving example of the use of the famous assumed name and anagram.

*Gift of Mrs. Chase Mellen, Jr., 1956.*

*Autograph letter signed [London, 7 October 1726] to Alexander Pope. 1 p.*
*23 x 17 cm.*

The only surviving letter from Voltaire to Pope. Voltaire's English is surprisingly good and the charm of his style survives in the alien tongue. He sends his good wishes to Pope who had been injured in a carriage accident. The Library has one of the largest institutional collections of the letters of Voltaire, including many written to his niece, Mme Denis.

*Purchased as the gift of the Fellows, 1960.*

Sir

I fear this moment of your sad adventure, that
water you fell in, was not the hyppocrene water
of Berwide. it would have respected you

In Deed I am concern'd beyond expression for
the Injury you have done in and more for your
word. it is unjustifiable that those fingers which have
written the rape of the lock (and the Essay) which
have dress'd Homer so becomingly in an english...
should have been so barbarously treated. Let the hand
of Dennis or of your prelates be cut off. your is
sacred. I hope for you are now perfectly recover'd
rely your accident concerns me of much of all
the disasters. his Master ought to affect his
scholar. I am sincerely for with the admiration
whose your deserve

your most humble
servant Voltaire

to my lord Bolingbroke's house
Wednesday Friday at noon

---

a Chateray ce 12 juin

Milord

vous etes une divinité et qui jay recours ordinaire
ment dans mes tribulations. vous venez vous grain...
Refus vous m'aves preté deux chevaux. je vous
Demande apresent le moitié De cette grace, apres...
La charité De confier un de vos courriers au portour
Jamais l'honneur de vos courriers dans quelque...
jour, Je vous repouws pour me preter dechy
ual, par Donez moy De mon la liberté que
je prends De vous le Demander.
Je suis ervous avec bien Durespect Dela rennaillence...

Milord

comment fauril faire
Vostre tres humble et tres
pour avoir l'honneur de vous    Sot serviteur
voir ?                           Arouet de Voltaire

## 18

JOHANN SEBASTIAN BACH, 1685–1750

*"Der Herr ist mein getreuer Hirt." Cantata no. 112. Autograph manuscript. [1731]. 12 p. 34 x 21 cm.*

This cantata is one of three by Bach written for the Second Sunday after Easter (Misericordias Domini). It was first performed in Leipzig on 8 April 1731. The text is the version of the 23rd Psalm by Wolfgang Musculus (1497–1563), first published in 1533. Both the Epistle and the Gospel for the day concern sheep going astray and the Good Shepherd. Along with cantata no. 4, "Christ lag in Todesbanden," this is among the finest of Bach's cantatas based on hymns.

*The Mary Flagler Cary Music Collection, 1968.*

19

WOLFGANG AMADEUS MOZART, 1756–1791

*"Der Schauspieldirektor." Autograph manuscript of the full score. 1786. 84 p.*
*23 x 32 cm.*

Mozart composed this delightful one-act singspiel, or comic opera, for a royal evening of entertainment presented by Emperor Joseph II of Austria in February 1786. It took him just over two weeks to complete the work. The slender plot concerns an impresario's frustrated attempts to assemble a cast for an opera. Two sopranos vie for the prima donna's role and much amusing rivalry ensues, and some very good music. The libretto is by Gottlieb Stephanie, who is best remembered as the librettist for Mozart's *The Abduction from the Seraglio. Der Schauspieldirektor* (also known as *The Impresario*) is still frequently performed; the overture, the first page of which is reproduced here, is particularly well known. This is the only complete manuscript of a Mozart opera in the United States.

*Purchased for the Mary Flagler Cary Music Collection, 1972.*

## 20

THOMAS JEFFERSON, 1743–1826

*Two autograph letters signed, Lake Champlain, New York, and Bennington, Vermont, May and June 1791, to his daughter, Martha (Mrs. Thomas M. Randolph), and his son-in-law. 9 p. 21 x 17.5 cm.*

These letters written on birch bark by the future President describe the beauties of New York State—although Jefferson still prefers Virginia—and comment on the battlefield at Bennington; he sends his affectionate best wishes to his family. They are from a collection of 173 letters from Jefferson, almost all of them to his daughter, which the Library acquired directly from his great-great-granddaughter.

*Purchased in 1925.*

Bennington in Vermont June 5. 1791.

Dear Sir

... Mr. Madison & myself are so far on

the tour we had projected. we have visited

in the course of it the principal scenes of

Burgoyne's misfortunes, to wit the grounds

at Stillwater where the action of that name

was fought, and more northwardly the road —

where our ... so much blood to both

armies, the encampment at Saratoga &

ground where the British piled their arms,

the field of the battle of Bennington about 9

miles from this place. we have also visited

Forts William Henry, & George, Ticonderoga,

Crown point, &c. which have been scenes of blood

in a very early part of our history. we were

more pleased however with the Lake ...

... Lake George than Mr. ...

I wrote to Martha yesterday, whilst

lying on with George & the same ...

... George is afforded me that ... to it

mere ... Lake George with its companion

... to it beautiful water, ever saw forms ...

... tour of mountains, into a ... as

... its length, & ... 2 & 3 miles broad

finely interspersed with islands, its waters

of crystal & the mountain sides

covered with rich groves ... things which ...

white pine, is however never broken ...

... trout ... we ... there ...

... to checquer the scene ...

... salmon trout, ... other fish ...

which it stored, have added to its ...

other amusements. the sport ...

21

SAMUEL TAYLOR COLERIDGE, 1772–1834

*Autograph letter signed [London, postmarked 29 December 1794] to Robert Southey. 3 p. with address. 38 x 23 cm.*

This is one of ninety-two letters written by Coleridge to Southey in the period 1794 to 1819. The earlier letters, such as this one, are effusive and contain many fair copies of Coleridge's poems. This letter was written after Coleridge's final rejection by his great love, Mary Evans. The Morgan Library has the largest single holding of Coleridge's autograph letters.

*Purchased with the assistance of the Fellows, 1957.*

I am calm, dear Southey! as an Autumnal Day, when the Sky is covered with grey moveless Clouds. To love her Habit has made unalterable: I had placed her in the sanctuary of my Heart, nor can she be torn from thence but with the Strings that grapple it to Life. This Passion however, divested as it now is of all Shadow of Hope, seems to lose its disquieting Power. Far distant, and never more to behold or hear of her, I shall sojourn in the Vale of Men sad and in loneliness, yet not unhappy. He cannot be long wretched who dares be actively virtuous. I am well assured, that she loves me as a favorite Brother. When she was present, she was to me only as a very dear Sister. it was in absence, that I felt those gnawings of Suspense, and that Dreaminess of Mind, which evidence an affection more restless, yet heavenly & pure, than fraternal. The Struggle has been well nigh too much for me — but, praised be the All-merciful! the feebleness of exhausted Feelings has produced a Calm, and my Heart stagnates into Peace.

Southey! my ideal Standard of female Excellence rises not above that Woman. But all Things work together for Good. Had I been united to her, the Excess of my Affection would have effeminated my Intellect. I should have fed on her Looks as she entered into the Room — I should have gazed on her Footsteps when she went out from me.

To lose her! — I can rise above that selfish Pang. But to marry another — O Southey! bear with my weakness. Love makes all things pure and heavenly like itself: — but to marry a woman whom I do not love — to degrade her, whom I call my Wife, by making her the Instrument of low Desire — and on the removal of a desultory Appetite, to be perhaps not displeased with her Absence! — Enough! — These Refinements are the wildering Fires, that lead me into Vice.

Mark you, Southey! — I will do my Duty.

I have this moment received your Letter. My Friend — you want but one Quality of Mind to be a — perfect Character—. Your Sensibilities are tempestuous — you feel Indignation at Weakness — now Indignation is the handsome Brother of Anger & Hatred — his Looks are "lovely in Terror" — yet still remember, who are his Relations. I would ardently, that you were a Necessitarian — and (believing in an all-loving Omnipotence) an Optimist. That puny Imp of Darkness yclept Scepticism — how could it dare to approach the hallowed Fires, that burn so brightly on the Altar of your Heart?

Think you, I wish to stay in Town? I am all eagerness to leave it — and am resolved, whatever be the consequence, to be at Bath by Saturday — I thought of walking down.

I have written to Bristol — and said, I could not assign a particular Time for my leaving Town — I spoke indefinitely that I might

JANE AUSTEN, 1775–1817

*"Lady Susan." Autograph manuscript of a novel left complete but unpublished and without title at the author's death. A fair copy, almost free from corrections and revisions, written on 158 pages (seventy-nine leaves), two of which have the date 1805 in the watermark. 19 x 15.5 cm.*

*Lady Susan* is a brief epistolary novel probably written about 1795, although Dr. R. W. Chapman dated it about 1805, observing that Jane Austen's handling of the story is "very unlike a novice." The novel was first published in 1871.

*Purchased in 1947.*

Letter 31.

Lady Susan to M.rs Johnson

Upper Seymour S.t

My dear Friend,

That tormenting Creature Reginald is
here. My Letter which was intended to keep him
longer in the Country, has hastened him to Town.
Much as I wish him away however, I cannot help
being pleased with such a proof of attachment. He
is devoted to me, heart & soul. — He will carry
this note himself, which is to serve as an Intro-
:duction to you, with whom he longs to be ac-
:quainted. Allow him to spend the Evening with
you, that I may bee in no danger of his return-
:ing here. — I have told him that I am not quite
well, & must be alone — & should he call again
there might be confusion, for it is impossible to
be sure of Servants. — Keep him therefore

23

WILLIAM BLAKE, 1757–1827

*"The Pickering Manuscript." Autograph manuscript unsigned.* [*c.1807*].
*22 p. 18.5 x 12 cm.*

The manuscript includes ten poems written about 1802–1804 and is the unique source for seven of them; it is a fair copy transcribed by Blake in or after 1807. For many years it has been known as "The Pickering Manuscript" because it was formerly owned by B. M. Pickering (1836–1878), who continued his father's traditions as publisher. The poems are well known to everyone who loves Blake's poetry, but the manuscript itself has rarely been seen and little studied. It was published in facsimile by the Morgan Library in 1972, with an introduction by Charles Ryskamp.

*Gift of Mrs. Landon K. Thorne, 1971.*

Thy Brother has armd himself in Steel
To avenge the wrongs thy Children feel

But vain the Sword & vain the Bow
They never can work Wars overthrow
The Hermits Prayer & the Widows tear
Alone can free the World from fear

For a Tear is an Intellectual Thing
And a Sigh is the Sword of an Angel King
And the bitter groan of the Martyrs woe
Is an arrow from the Almighties Bow

The hand of Vengeance found the Bed
To which the Purple Tyrant fled
The iron hand crushd the Tyrants head
And became a Tyrant in his Stead

### Auguries of Innocence

To see a World in a Gram of Sand
And a Heaven in a Wild Flower
Hold Infinity in the palm of your hand
And Eternity in an hour
A Robin Red breast in a Cage
Puts all Heaven in a Rage
A dove house filld with Doves & Pigeons

LUDWIG VAN BEETHOVEN, 1770–1827

*Trio, piano and strings, op. 70, no. 1, D major. Autograph manuscript. 1808.*
*65 p. 24 x 31 cm.*

Beethoven composed the two trios for piano and strings, op. 70, in Vienna in 1808. They are dedicated to Countess Marie Erdödy, an accomplished pianist and enthusiastic admirer of Beethoven and his music. He was living in her house when he composed the trios, and they were first performed there in the Christmas season of 1808. Beethoven later quarrelled with the Countess and, in May 1809, he asked his publisher, Breitkopf & Härtel, to change the dedication if it were not too late. The music had already been published, so the dedication remained. (Beethoven had asked that the new dedicatee be Archduke Rudolph; he, of course, was later honored with the Trio in B flat, op. 97— known as the "Archduke Trio.") Our Trio is popularly called the "Geister" (or "Ghost"), a reference to the gloomy, hushed character of the second movement.

*The Mary Flagler Cary Music Collection, 1968.*

25

WILLIAM WORDSWORTH, 1775–1850

*Autograph letter signed [Keswick, November 1811], to Sir George Beaumont.*
*3 p. with address. 39.5 x 25 cm.*

Wordsworth was one of the many friends of the artist and collector Sir George Beaumont. And this letter is one of several hundred to Sir George from a score of poets, artists, and other gifted acquaintances that have come to us with the Coleorton Papers. Wordsworth here writes out, with a few corrections, an inscription he had written for an urn which is to be placed at the termination of a newly planted avenue, in memory of Sir Joshua Reynolds.

*Purchased as the gift of the Fellows, 1954.*

My dear Sir George,

Had there been room at the end of the small avenue of Lime trees, for planting a spatious circle of the same trees, The Urn might have been placed in the ?centre & the Inscription thus altered.

Ye Lime trees, ranged around this hallowed Urn,
Shoot forth with lively power at Spring's return!
And be not slow a stately growth to rear,
Bending your docile boughs from year to year,
Till in a solemn Concave they unite;
Like that Cathedral Dome beneath whose height
Reynolds, among our Country's noble Dead,
In the last sanctity of fame is laid.

— There though, by right, the excelling Painter sleep,
Where Death and Glory a joint sabbath keep,
Yet not the less his Spirit would hold dear
Self-hidden praise, and Friendship's private tears;
And, on my native grounds, unblamed may I
Raise this frail Tribute to his memory;
From youth, a zealous Follower of the Art
That he profess'd — attached to him in heart;
Admiring, loving, and with grief and pride
Feeling what England lost when Reynolds died.

_____ for the Stone near the Cedar, thus altered.
See the margin

Planted by Beaumont and by Wordsworth's hands.
One wooed the silent Art with studious pains,
These Groves have heard the Other's pensive strains;
Devoted thus their Spirits did unite
By interchange of knowlege and delight.
May Nature's kindliest Powers sustain the Tree,
And Love protect it from all injury!

## 26

DOMINIQUE JEAN LARREY, BARON, 1766–1842

*"Field Diary. Russia." 4 February 1812 to 1 October 1813. 125 p. 17.5 x 20 cm.*

In this diary the Surgeon-in-Chief of the French army under Napoleon recounts his experiences with the "Grande Armée" during the Russian campaign and the retreat from Moscow. It is a remarkable relic of the military catastrophe. His graphic accounts of the suffering in intense cold, the hunger, and the natural disasters that befell the army fill the reader with horror. Throughout the diary Larrey tells of his concern for the sick and the wounded. He is credited with the invention of the field ambulance, but he had little chance to use it in this campaign. In his will Napoleon left Larrey a legacy and called him "The most virtuous man I have known."

*Gift of Mrs. George H. Fitch, 1967.*

l'intérêt personnel était le seul mobile de tous les individus de l'armée - le pied ne connaissait plus le frère, le main ne portait plus aucune attention à la femme qui avait partagé jusqu'à lors ses privations et ses fatigues, les enfants eux mêmes, étaient délaissés; enfin la nature ne connaissait plus aucun de ses droits. je fus frappé à l'approche de Smolensk à la vue d'une jeune femme pressée par la faim dévorante elle se jette à travers un groupe de soldats qui venaient d'éventrer un cheval couverte d'une pelisse de martre garnie de satin blanc, plonge ses mains dans le ventre de l'animal pour en arracher le foie ou quelques unes de ses portions, mais privée de couteau elle est obligée d'employer ses dents dont elle se sert en les plongeant dans le ventre même du cheval, enfin elle emporte un morceau de la victime et court le faire cuire au 1er feu de bivouac qu'elle rencontre - sans doute qu'elle n'a attendu sa parfaite cuisson pour le manger - hélas! combien de ces malheureuses femmes n'ont elles pas succombé aux effets terribles de ce besoin impérieux. dans un autre moment je tâcherai d'expliquer le phénomène de le sentiment (la faim). Cependant cette faible ressource de la viande de cheval quelque peu de farine qu'une partie de l'armée avait conservé quelques legumes ou des morceaux de pain ou de salé qu'une autre était parvenue dans les campagnes éloignées de la route et l'espoir de trouver des magazins à Smolensk nous soutinrent. enfin l'on arrive à cette ville tant désirée - le froid était très vif et le mercure était descendu dans le thermomètre à 14 degrés

mais qu'elle surprise pénible, à peine trouvât-on des subsistances pour le petit nombre [...] entrer dans cette place, et les malades des hôp[itaux] l'impérieuse nécessité fait forcer les portes et les magazins sont pillés - un petit nombre profite du pillage pour quelque temps mais le reste de l'armée est condamné à souffrir. déja les malades sont privés des distributions accoutumées pendant deux jours que nous séjournâmes dans cette ville j'eus la douleur de voir nos blessés et mes off[iciers] de toute subsistance aucune - je partageai avec une 30[aine] de ces derniers un sac de farine que j'avais pu acheter à grand prix, c'est la seule ressource que nous eûmes pour traverser encore un grand espace de déserts. mon âme resta encore épouvantée des effets d'attirants et horribles que fit sur elle l'ambulance établie de la brèche placée à la porte du Niéper - les malheureux étaient dans une situation plus affreuse dans cette ambulance que dans celle de Koloskoï - dans les autres hôp[itaux] les malades étaient moins mal - mais nous ne pouvons en tramer aucun faute de transports d'ailleurs le temps déjà très rigoureux - mes efforts furent inutiles et pour faire assurer l'existence de ces malheureux et pour les préserver des flammes au moins de l'ambulance désignée voisine de l'anticipation que l'on fit à notre départ. les autres hôpitaux auraient été sauvés étant éloignés, et construits en pierre néanmoins la ville était en feu à notre départ

## 27

SIR WALTER SCOTT, BART., 1771–1832

*"The Antiquary." Autograph manuscript. 3 vols. 1816. 26.5 x 19 cm.*

This novel is generally believed to have been Scott's favorite among his own works. It tells of the love of William Lovel for the daughter of Sir Arthur Wardour in the time of George III. The collection of the manuscripts of Scott's novels, poems, and letters in the Library is the largest known, and "The Antiquary" was a splendid addition.

*Purchased in 1929.*

# The Antiquary
## Chapter I.

Go call a coach and let a coach be called
And let the man who calleth be the caller
And in his calling let him nothing call
But Coach! Coach! Coach! O for a coach ye Gods!"

*Chrononhotontholozos*

It was early in the ~~morning~~ of a fine summers day when a young man

near the end of the eighteenth century

of ~~very~~ genteel appearance having occasion to go towards the NorthEast of Scotland provided himself with a ticket in one of those public carriages which travel between Edinburgh and the Queensferry; at which place as the name implies, there is a passage-boat for crossing the Firth of Forth. The ~~vehicle~~ coach was calculated to carry six regular passengers besides such interlopers as the Coachman could pick up by the way and intrude upon those who were legally in possession. The tickets which conferred right to a seat in this vehicle of little-ease were dispensed by a sharp-looking old dame with a pair of spectacles on a very thin nose who inhabited a "laigh shop" anglicè a cellar, opening to the High street by a strait and steep stair at the bottom of which she sold tape thread needles skeins of worsted coarse linen cloth and such feminine gear to those who had the courage & skill to descend to the profundity of her dwelling without

falling

~~tumbling~~ themselves or throwing down any of the numerous articles which piled on each side of the descent indicated the profession of the trader below.

written

The handbill which published on a projecting board announced that the Queensferry Diligence or Hawes Fly departed precisely at twelve o'clock on Tuesday the fifteenth July 17— in order to secure for the travellers the opportunity of passing the Firth with the tide

flood

lied upon the present occasion like a bulletin. For although that hour was pealed from Saint Giles's steeple and repeated by the Tron no coach appeared upon the appointed stand. It is true only two tickets had been taken out & possibly the last of the subterranean manager might have an understanding with her Automedon that in such cases a little space was to be allowed for the chance of filling up the vacant places — or the said

## 28

CARL MARIA VON WEBER, 1786–1826

*"Aufforderung zum Tanze." Rondo for piano, op. 65. Autograph manuscript signed, 28 July 1819. 4 p. 24 x 32.5 cm.*

With this composition, also known as "Invitation to the Dance," Weber became the first composer to write a waltz-sequence, a form of composition brought to its highest peak of development by Johann Strauss, Jr. The work was orchestrated by Berlioz and performed as ballet music in 1841 in a Paris production of Weber's *Der Freischütz*. It is in this orchestral version that the work is best known today. This is the only recorded complete manuscript of the composition for piano.

*Purchased for the Mary Flagler Cary Music Collection, 1973, and in honor of the Fiftieth Anniversary of the Library.*

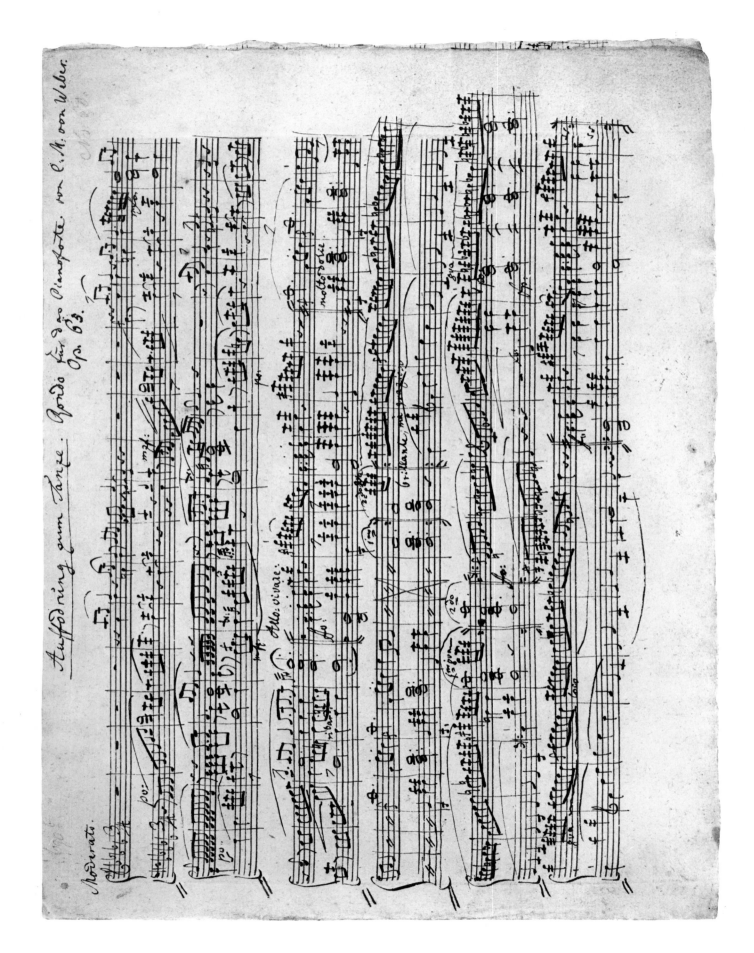

## 29

FRANZ PETER SCHUBERT, 1797–1828

*"Die Winterreise." Autograph manuscript signed. 1827. 74 p. 24.5 x 31.5 cm.*

These twenty-four songs form what is generally considered the greatest song cycle ever written. The first part, consisting of the twelve songs dated February 1827, contains many corrections and revisions. It is probable that Schubert considered this to be the complete cycle and only later came across the entire set of Wilhelm Müller's poems—twenty-four in all. The second part, with the additional twelve songs, is dated October 1827; it is a fair copy throughout. Both parts were published by Haslinger of Vienna, Part I in January 1828; Part II in December after Schubert's death. Among the other Schubert manuscripts in the Library is that of another great song cycle, *Schwanengesang*.

*Purchased for the Mary Flagler Cary Music Collection, 1968.*

30

HECTOR BERLIOZ, 1803–1869

*"Le roi de Thulé. Chanson gothique de Faust." Autograph manuscript.* [*1828*].
*4 p. 30 x 23 cm.*

"Another landmark in my life," writes Berlioz in his *Memoirs*, "was my first encounter with Goethe's *Faust*, which I read in Gérard de Nerval's translation, and which made a strange and deep impression on me. The marvellous book fascinated me from the first." Berlioz probably read *Faust* sometime in 1827; the earliest reference in his correspondence is in a letter of 16 September 1828, which speaks of "Shakespeare and Goethe, mentors of my life, mute confidants of my grief!" and which goes on: "The day before yesterday, while travelling, I wrote the ballad of the King of Thulé." Seven more pieces were composed during the next few months, and the whole published as *Huit scènes de Faust* in April 1829. Berlioz also used the song in his *La Damnation de Faust*, first performed in 1846. This manuscript is part of a large collection of autograph musical manuscripts presented to the Library by Mr. Lehman during the past few years.

*Gift of Mr. Robert O. Lehman, 1972.*

31

CHARLOTTE BRONTË, 1816–1855

*Autograph manuscript notebook of poetry and prose. 1830. 12 p. 18.5 x 12.5 cm.*

Two pages from the notebook are shown here, one with the poem which begins, "True pleasure breathes not city air." This notebook is part of The Henry Houston Bonnell Brontë Collection, which had been on deposit in the Library since 1963, and was bequeathed to the Library in the estate of Mrs. Bonnell, who died in 1969. The Collection contains many poetical and prose manuscripts by the three Brontë sisters, by their brother, Patrick Branwell, and some materials relating to their father.

*Bequest of Mrs. Henry Houston Bonnell, 1969.*

## 32

FRÉDÉRIC FRANÇOIS CHOPIN, 1810–1849

*Étude, piano, op. 10, no. 7, C major. Autograph manuscript. [1832]. 2 p. 26 x 35 cm.*

The twenty-four études of Chopin, twelve each in op. 10 and op. 25, explore virtually every facet of the pianist's technique. The first set, op. 10, was dedicated to Franz Liszt and was published in 1833. No. 7, the first page of which is reproduced here, is based on alternating thirds and sixths in the right hand. It was composed in the spring of 1832. Like all of the Chopin études it is not only a technical study but an attractive and original composition as well. The manuscript comes from the collection of Ernest Schelling, the American pianist, composer, and conductor, who studied piano at the Paris Conservatoire with George Mathias, who had himself been a pupil of Chopin.

*Gift of Mrs. Janos Scholz, 1965.*

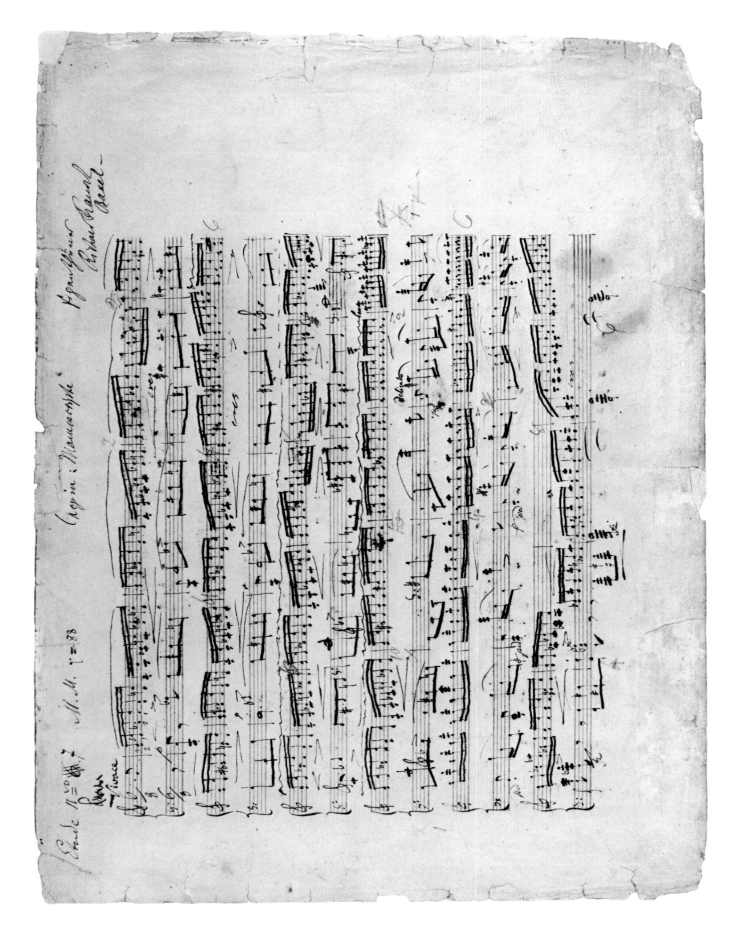

## 33

HONORÉ DE BALZAC, 1799–1850

*"Eugénie Grandet." Autograph manuscript and corrected galley proofs signed,*
*24 December 1833. 157 leaves. 27 x 20 cm.*

Balzac presented this manuscript of one of his greatest and most popular novels to Mme Eveline de Hanska on her birthday in 1833, at which time he had known her for about three months. They remained friends throughout Balzac's life and were married shortly before his death. The manuscript is a tortuous mass of rapid writing, corrections, and additions with forty-one leaves of corrected galley proofs of the first chapter bound in; it reflects the energy and exuberance with which Balzac worked, but could not have filled his typesetters with enthusiasm. The work represents a most important period in the career of the man whom some authorities consider the greatest novelist of all time. To the best of our knowledge, it is the only major Balzac manuscript not in a French collection.

*Purchased in 1925.*

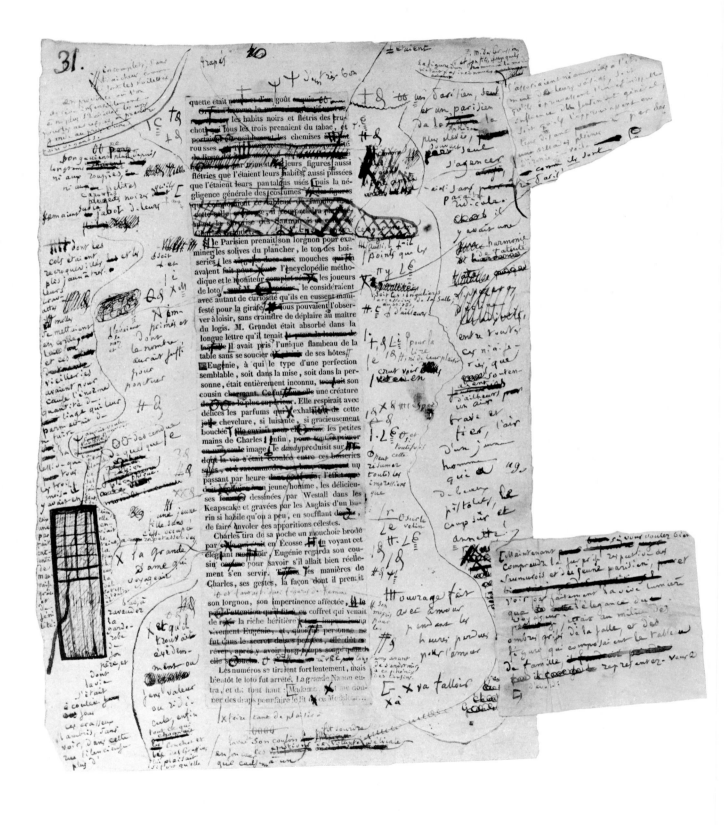

HENRY DAVID THOREAU, 1817–1862

*"Journal, Vol. III." Autograph manuscript 1840–1841. 135 p. 19 x 15 cm.*

Thoreau kept from the age of twenty a remarkable record of his life and mind. This record, a Journal of nearly two million words in thirty-nine volumes, was preserved in a stout box of yellow pine, made by Thoreau. J. Pierpont Morgan purchased this Journal manuscript in 1909; unfortunately, Volume III, which covers the period from 30 July 1840 through 22 January 1841, had become separated from the other volumes sometime before Morgan acquired the set. It was not until 1956 that the "lost" notebook was reunited with its companion volumes in the Library. Many extracts from this volume went into the making of Thoreau's first book, *A Week on the Concord and Merrimack Rivers*, and a few comments on Walden Pond in winter found their way into *Walden*. The complete "lost" Journal was edited by Perry Miller and published as *Consciousness in Concord* (Boston, 1958).

*Purchased as a gift of the Fellows, with the special assistance of Mr. C. Waller Barrett, Mrs. Louis M. Rabinowitz, and Mr. Robert H. Taylor, 1956.*

Sunday Dec. 27th 1840

The wood gaily wears its burden of snow. It is glad and warm always, sometimes even more genial in winter than in summer. The snow melts round every tree.

In a little hollow between the hills, some twenty feet higher than the village, lies Walden pond, the expressed juice of the hills and trees whose leaves are annually steeped in it. Its history is in the lapse of its waves, in the rounded pebbles on its shore, and the pines which have grown on its bank.

It has its precessions and recessions, its cycles and epicycles — it has not been idle, though sedentary as Abu Musa — who says that "Sitting still at home is the heavenly way, the going out is the way of the world." Yet in its evaporations and by a thousand unimagined ways it has travelled as far as any.

35

RICHARD DOYLE, 1824–1883

*"Beauty and the Beast." Manuscript signed. 1842. 36 p. 25 x 18.5 cm.*

About 1842, Adelaide Doyle made a translation of the story of "Beauty and the Beast," and her brother Richard ("Dick") illustrated it with some delightful pen drawings. This manuscript has now joined our collection of children's literature, and was published by the Library in 1973, with an introduction by Charles Ryskamp. Doyle became one of the greatest Victorian illustrators, and this early work contains all the elements of his genius.

*Purchased for the Elisabeth Ball Collection, 1971.*

# BEAUTY AND THE BEAST,

There was once upon a time a merchant who was extremely rich. He had six children, three boys, and three girls, and as he was an intellectual man he spared nothing in the education of his children, and gave them all sorts of masters. His daughters were very beautiful, but the youngest was especially admired, and when she was little she was called the beautiful

36

JOHN RUSKIN, 1819–1900

*Autograph letter signed [Chamonix, 24 June 1849] to his wife, Effie Gray Ruskin. 4 p. with address. 22.5 x 18 cm.*

Ruskin and Euphemia (Effie) Gray were married in April 1848; the marriage was annulled in 1854. With ignorance typical of the age, neither John nor Effie seems to have known exactly what to expect in a normal marriage relationship. This letter was written from Switzerland a year after the marriage, while Effie was with her parents in Scotland and John was travelling in Europe with his parents. Effie had recently written him an especially affectionate letter and he answers consenting half-heartedly to a little Alice or a little Effie of their own. "Only I wish they weren't so small at first that one hardly knows what one has got hold of." Many years later, Effie did have both an Alice and an Effie of her own, but they were children by her second husband, John Millais. This letter is from the Bowerswell Papers which document the marriage and much more in the lives of the Ruskin and Gray families. The Library also has the papers of Millais and a large collection of Ruskin's correspondence.

*Purchased as the gift of the Fellows, 1950.*

Sunday Evening

My darling Effie.

I have been thinking of you a great deal in my walks to day. as of course I always do when I am not busy. but when I am measuring or drawing mountains, I forget myself — and my wife both; if I did not I could not stop so long away from her, for I begin to wonder whether I am married at all. and to think of all my happy hours, and soft slumber in my dearest lady's arms, as a dream — However I feel in such cases. for my last, letter and look at the signature. and see that it is all right. I got one on Friday; that in which you tell me you are better — thank God; and that your father is so much happier. and that Alice is so winning and that you would like a little Alice of our own. so should I; a little Effie. at least. Only I wish they weren't so small at first that one hardly knows what one has got hold of: I have to thank you also very much for what you say about Vevay: &c: Your father writes to me that he thinks one winter there would cure me of my fancy; I wonder if he thinks that I am in the habit of taking "fancies" of so serious a nature, without remembering that there is such a thing as winter — or whether he supposes I should be willing to leave my country, and my friends; and all the advantages I have in London, for a fancy of any kind: However, you may as well assure him that winter, when the vine grows wild, is a very endurable season,

37

NATHANIEL HAWTHORNE, 1804–1864

*"Tanglewood Tales for Girls and Boys. Being a Second Wonder Book."*
*Autograph manuscript signed, Concord, Mass., 1853. 146 leaves. 25 x 20 cm.*

To our collection of Hawthorne manuscripts, the largest in any library, the manuscript of *Tanglewood Tales* was a most welcome addition, for it was written expressly for children. A sequel to *A Wonder-Book*, it is also a retelling of Greek myths for young people; Hawthorne took great pleasure in reading the stories to his own children. The manuscript is a valuable acquisition for our collection of American literary manuscripts and for our growing collection of children's literature.

*Purchased as the gift of the Fellows, 1964–1965.*

# The Minotaur.

In the old city of Trœzene, at the foot of a lofty mountain, there lived, a very long time ago, a little boy named Theseus. His grandfather, King Pittheus, was the sovereign of that country, and was reckoned a very wise man; so that Theseus, being brought up in the royal palace, and being naturally a bright lad, could hardly fail of profiting by the old king's instructions. His mother's name was Æthra. As for his father, the boy had never seen him. But, from his earliest remembrance, Æthra used to go with little Theseus into a wood, and sit down upon a moss-grown rock, which was deeply sunken into the earth. Here she often talked with her son about his father, and said that he was called Ægeus, and that he was a great king, and ruled over Attica, and dwelt at Athens, which was as famous a city as any in the world. Theseus was very fond of hearing about King Ægeus, and often asked his good mother Æthra why he did not come and live with them, at Trœzene.

"Ah, my dear son," answered Æthra, with a sigh, "a monarch has his people to take care of. The men and women, over whom he rules, are in the place of children to him; and he can seldom spare time to love his own children, as other parents do. Your father will never be able to leave his kingdom, for the sake of seeing his little boy."

"Well, but dear mother," asked the boy, "why cannot I go to this famous city of Athens, and tell King Ægeus that I am his son?"

"That may happen, by-and-by," said Æthra. "Be patient, and we shall see. You are not yet big and strong enough to set out on such an errand."

"And how soon shall I be strong enough?" Theseus persisted in inquiring.

"You are but a tiny boy as yet," replied his mother. "See if you can lift this rock on which we are sitting!"

The little fellow had a great opinion of his own strength. So, grasping the rough protuberances of the rock, he tugged and toiled amain, and got himself quite out of breath, without being able to

38

HERMAN MELVILLE, 1819–1891

*Autograph letter signed, Pittsfield, Mass., 24 November 1853, to Harper &*
*Brothers. 1 p. 22 x 17 cm.*

About 1896 a member of the staff of Harper & Brothers made a selection of letters from
the correspondence files of the firm. These letters, numbering about 1250, were from
many prominent authors, artists, and public figures whose works were published by
Harpers. This selection disappeared, and was only rediscovered in the 1950s; it is now
in the Morgan Library. Included are eight letters from Herman Melville of which one
is reproduced here. It concerns a book on "Tortoises and Tortoise Hunting," for which
Melville received an advance (despite the "declined" marked on the letter), but which
was never completed.

*Gift of Harper & Brothers, 1958.*

Pittsfield Nov 24th 1853

Gentlemen : — In addition to the work which I took to New York last Spring, but which I was prevented from printing at that time; I have now on hand, and pretty well on towards completion, another book — 300 pages, say — partly of nautical adventure, and partly — or rather, chiefly, of Tortoise Hunting Adventure. It will be ready for press some time in the coming January. Meanwhile, it would be convenient, to have advances to me upon it $300. — My acct: with you, at present, can not be very far from square. For the abovenamed advance — if remitted me now — you will have security in my former works, as well as security prospective, in the one to come, ( The Tortoise-Hunters ) because if you accede to the aforesaid request; this letter shall be your voucher, that I am willing your house should publish it, on the old basis — half-profits.

Reply immediately, if you please,

And Believe Me, Yours

Herman Melville

39

RICHARD WAGNER, 1813–1883

*"Die Meistersinger von Nürnberg." Autograph manuscript signed of the libretto for the opera. [1862]. 82 p. 29 x 23 cm.*

The manuscript of what has been called "the greatest libretto ever written" was completed in January 1862 and published at the end of that year. Wagner did not finish the full score of the opera until 1867. In the course of musical composition Wagner introduced many textual changes (some small, some of major significance) and it is revealing to compare this libretto in its early version with the form it finally assumed in the published score. The proof sheets of *Die Meistersinger*, heavily corrected by Wagner, are in The Heineman Collection. This manuscript was formerly owned by Kaiser Wilhelm II who had a facsimile edition of it published in 1893. In 1909 it was in the library of George C. Thomas, a banker of Philadelphia, and a partner in Drexel, Morgan & Company of New York and other affiliated firms. There is an unauthenticated story that both Pierpont Morgan and Mr. Thomas admired the libretto when it was shown to them by the Kaiser. The latter caught the spirit of the admiration of his guests and offered to sell it to one of them—to be decided by the toss of a coin. Mr. Thomas won.

*Gift of Mr. Arthur A. Houghton, Jr., in honor of the Fiftieth Anniversary of the Library, 1974.*

## Erster Aufzug.

Die Bühne stellt das Innere der Katharinenkirche, in schrägem Durchschnitt, dar; von dem Hauptschiff, welches links ab dem Hintergrunde zu sich ausdehnend anzunehmen ist, sind nur noch die letzten Reihen der Kirchstuhlbänke sichtbar: den Vordergrund nimmt der freie Raum vor dem Chor ein; dieser wird später durch einen Vorhang, gegen das Schiff zu gänzlich abgeschlossen.

Beim Aufzug hört man, unter Orgelbegleitung, von der Gemeinde den letzten Vers eines Chorales, mit welchem der Nachmittagsgottesdienst zur Einleitung des Johannisfestes schliesst, singen. Während des Chorales und dessen Zwischenspielen, entwickelt sich, vom Orchester begleitet, folgende pantomimische Scene:

In der letzten Reihe der Kirchstühle sitzen Eva und Magdalene; Walther von Stolzing steht, in einiger Entfernung, zur Seite an eine Säule gelehnt, die Blicke auf Eva heftend. Eva dreht sich wiederholt seitwärts nach dem Ritter um, und erwidert seine dringend bittenden Gebärden mit verlegenen Winken, die ihm bedeuten sollen, er möge beim Ausgange ihrer harren. Magdalene unterbricht sich öfter im Gesang, um Eva zu zupfen und zur Vorsicht zu mahnen. – Als der Choral zu Ende ist, und, während eines längeren Orgelnachspieles, die Gemeinde dem Hauptausgange, welcher links dem Hintergrund zu anzunehmen ist, sich zuwendet, um allmählich die Kirche zu verlassen, tritt Walther an die beiden Frauen, welche sich ebenfalls von ihren Sitzen erhoben haben und dem Ausgange sich zuwenden wollen, lebhaft heran.

F Choral der Gemeinde.

Da zu dir der Heiland kam,
willig deine Taufe nahm,
weihte sich dem Opfertod,
gab er uns des Heil's Gebot:
dass wir durch dein' Tauf' uns weih'n,
seines Opfer's werth zu sein.
Edler Täufer!
Christ's Vorläufer!
Nimm uns freundlich an!
dort am Fluss Jordan.

**Walther**
(leise, doch feurig zu Eva.)

Verweilt! – Ein Wort! Ein einzig Wort!

**Eva**
(sich rasch zu Magdalene wendend.)

Mein Brusttuch! Schau! Wohl liegt's im Ort?

**Magdalene**

Vergesslich Kind! Nun heisst es: such'!
(Sie kehrt nach den Sitzen zurück.)

**Walther**

Fräulein! Verzeiht der Sitte Bruch!
Eines zu wissen, eines zu fragen,
was nicht müsst' ich zu brechen wagen:
Ob Leben oder Tod? Ob Segen oder Fluch?
mit einem Worte sei mir's vertraut: –
mein Fräulein, sagt –

**Magdalene**
(zurückkommend.)

Hier ist das Tuch.

## 40

CHARLES DICKENS, 1812–1870

*"Our Mutual Friend." Autograph manuscript signed. 1865. 2 vols. 23 x 19 cm.*

Although it lacks the spontaneity of his earlier works, this novel is considered by many critics to be one of Dickens' best because of his acute concern with upper-middle-class society and its social responsibilities. Dickens "plotted" the novel carefully and his "plottings" are bound in the front of each of these volumes. He also made innumerable erasures and corrections before sending this manuscript to the printer.

*Purchased in 1944.*

In Four Books.

Book the First. ———— The Cup and the Lip.

## Chapter I

On the Look Out

In these times of ours, though concerning the exact year there is no need to be precise, a boat of dirty and disreputable appearance, with two figures in it, floated on the Thames, between Southwark Bridge which is of iron, and London Bridge which is of stone, as an autumn evening was closing in.

The figures in this boat were those of a strong man with ragged grizzled hair and a sun-browned face, and a girl of nineteen or twenty, sufficiently like him to be recognizable as his daughter. The girl rowed, pulling a pair of sculls very easily; and the man, with the rudder-lines slack in his hands, and his hands loose in his waistband, kept an eager look-out. He had no net, hook, or line, and could not be a fisherman; his boat had no cushion for a sitter, no paint, no inscription, no appliance beyond a rusty boathook and a coil of rope, and he could not be a waterman; his boat was too crazy and too small to take in cargo for delivery, and he could not be a lighterman or river-carrier; there was no clue to what he looked for, but he looked for something, with a most intent and searching gaze. The tide, which had turned an hour before, was running down, and his eyes watched every little race and eddy in its broad sweep, as the boat made slight head-way against it, or drove stern foremost before it, according as he directed his daughter by a movement of his head. She watched his face as earnestly as he watched the river. But, in the intensity of her look there was a touch of dread or horror.

Allied to the bottom of the river rather than the surface, by reason of the slime and ooze with which it was covered, and its sodden state, this boat and the two figures in it obviously were doing something that they often did, and were seeking what they often sought. Half savage as the man showed, with no covering on his matted head, with his brown arms bare to between the elbow and the shoulder, with the loose knot of a looser kerchief lying low on his bare breast in a wilderness of beard and whisker, with such dress as he wore seeming to be made out of the mud that begrimed his boat, still there was a business-like usage in his steady gaze. So with every lithe action of the girl, with every turn of her wrist, perhaps most of all with her look of dread or horror; they were things of usage.

"Keep her out, Lizzie. Tide runs strong here. Keep her well afore the sweep of it."

Trusting to the girl's skill and making no adaptation of himself to the boat, he sat still and certain. So the girl eyed him. But, it happened now, that a slant of light from the setting sun glanced into the bottom of the boat, and, touching a rotten stain there which bore some resemblance to the outline of a muffled human form, coloured it as if with diluted blood. This caught the girl's eye, and she shivered.

"What ails you?" said the man, immediately aware of it, though so intent on the advancing waters; "I see nothing afloat."

The red light was gone, the shudder was gone, and his gaze, which had come back to the boat for a moment, travelled away again. Wheresoever the strong tide met with an impediment, his gaze paused for an instant. At every mooring-chain and rope, at every stationary boat or barge that split the current into a broken-up roll of water, at the paddles of the river steamboats, as the rattling dip of oar and scull, his shining eyes darted a hungry look. After a darkening hour or so, suddenly the rudder-lines tightened in his hold, and he steered hard towards the Surrey shore.

## 41

ÉDOUARD MANET, 1832–1883

*Autograph letter signed, Paris, 15 January 1871, to his wife and to his mother.*
*4 p. 21 x 13.5 cm.*

During the Franco-Prussian War, the painter Édouard Manet served as a lieutenant in the Garde Nationale. His family had taken refuge in the Pyrenees, but Manet was able to get letters to them even during the siege of Paris. We now have thirty of these autograph letters written to his wife and mother in 1870 and 1871. Paper was scarce during the siege and Manet uses the sheets fully as this reproduction shows. He writes of the cold, the lack of food, and disease. In February 1871 Manet was able to leave Paris and was soon reunited with his family.

*Gift of Mrs. Henry T. Curtiss, 1971.*

bientôt j'espère — tu sais mon
chi mon meuble de l'heure — Aussi mon
maintenant malgré tout
se me deliaite
t'auras que j'en ai souffert et
avec l'autre — Maman n'aurait pas
de supporter le régime et l'ai ta
ment beaucoup de monde à Paris.
un ami est malade certainement il
d'espère que tu à conduite de deon
fui à bien soin de maman et de
sar je l'ai envoté avec ton pauvre
retrouver tu le l'on s'appelle par ia
beaucoup de garçon de son âge se bath
bien sullant — une Mr Manet a été tré
les sans — li par un obus vous me le nou
été mis dans une li sur à haza dans
tous ce j'aurai et que de pauvais
t'amber sucer nos yeux
se m'enpresse de tous
enlever

42

WILLIAM ERNEST HENLEY, 1849–1903

*"Invictus." Autograph manuscript draft of the poem, April 1875. 1 p. 26 x 20.5 cm.*

Henley is best remembered for his vigorous and unsentimental sketches of life as a patient in the Edinburgh Infirmary ("In Hospital"), and for his poem "Invictus," now perhaps somewhat tarnished by too frequent inclusion in anthologies. An immature and somewhat feeble version of "Invictus" is reproduced here to show the raw material from which a stirring lyric finally evolved. The Henley Archive contains drafts and early versions of many poems, a large collection of letters written to Henley, and much family correspondence. The Library also has many autograph manuscripts and letters of other authors of the late nineteenth and early twentieth centuries, including Ernest Dowson, Rossetti, Stevenson, Swinburne, and Wilde.

*Gift of Mr. Edwin J. Beinecke, 1955.*

This was a woman once. A ruined life
From all the shame, the horror & the strife
    Has turned for mercy to the silent river.

The loving thought of Death esteems her dear.
She has no more to suffer or to fear.
    Equal & free, she triumphs from the river.

The world wags on, with neither joy nor dole.
Wash from her lips the paint, as from her soul
    Her stain of life, O deep compassionate river.

                       = 7-8/4/75 =

= A Thanksgiving =
=

From brief delights that rise to me
    Out of unfathomable dole,
I thank whatever gods there be
    For mine unconquerable soul.

In the strong clutch of Circumstance
    It has not winced, nor groaned aloud.
Before the blows of cyclops Chance
    My head is bloody, but unbowed.

I front unfeared the threat of Space
    And dwindle into dark again.
My work is done, I take my place
    Among the years that wait for men.

My life, my broken life, must be
    One long unconquerable dole.
I thank the gods — They gave to me
    A dauntless & defiant soul.

                       = 9-10/4/75 =

43

JOHANNES BRAHMS, 1833–1897

*Symphony no. 1 in C minor, op. 68. Autograph manuscript of the full score (the first movement wanting). 94 p. 26 x 33.5 cm.*

Brahms began work on his first symphony in 1855 but did not complete the composition until 1876. The first movement was only partially completed as late as 1862. He resumed work on the symphony in 1874, adding the slow introduction and the last three movements, and completing it in September 1876. It was first performed on 4 November in Karlsruhe, and was conducted by Otto Dessoff from this manuscript. Brahms's first symphony is among the most frequently performed and recorded works in the orchestral repertory.

*The Mary Flagler Cary Music Collection, 1968.*

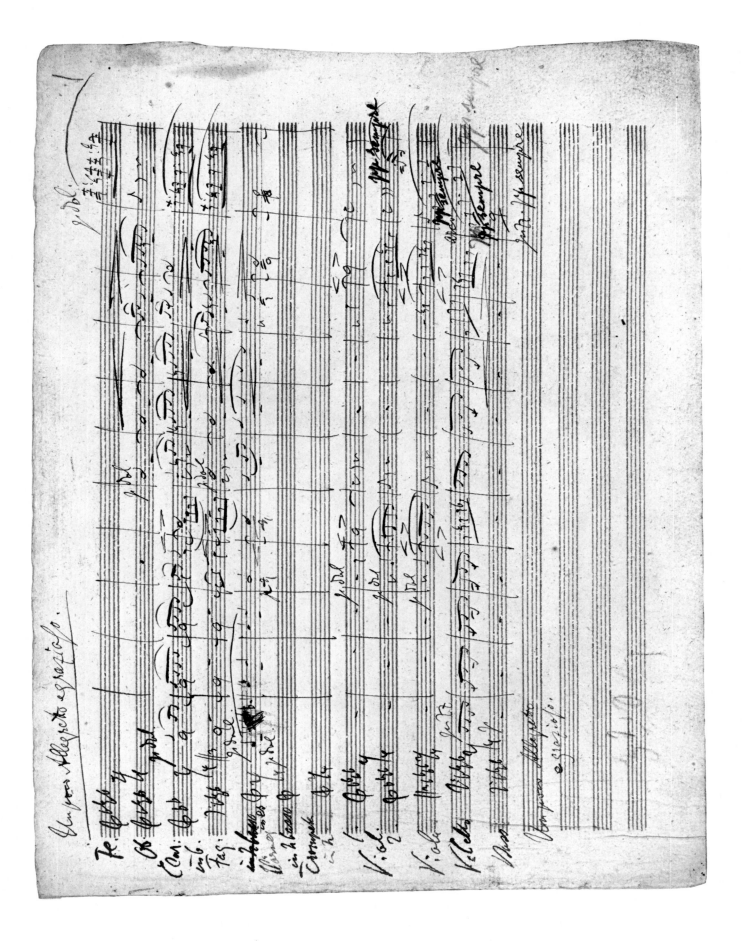

44

SIR ARTHUR SEYMOUR SULLIVAN, 1842–1900

*"The Pirates of Penzance." Autograph manuscript of the full score. 1879.*
*2 vols. 33 x 24 cm.*

*The Pirates of Penzance*, the fifth opera on which Gilbert and Sullivan collaborated, was unique for several reasons. It was the initial joint effort of the D'Oyly Carte Opera Company, the newly formed triumvirate of Gilbert, Sullivan, and Richard D'Oyly Carte. Further, it was the only one of their fourteen operas to have its world production première in America. The composer and dramatist were in New York in connection with a new production of *H. M. S. Pinafore*. Sullivan had prepared much of the music in England, but, having left this material behind, he had to rewrite from memory. The two men worked at a feverish pace and in due course the *Pirates* opened at the Fifth Avenue Theatre on 31 December 1879, before a highly enthusiastic audience. However, to protect the opera's British copyright, a single performance had been given twenty hours previously, on 30 December, at the Bijou Theatre, Paignton. On 3 April 1880, the *Pirates* had its third "première" in London at the Opera Comique, where it ran for 363 performances.

*Purchased in 1966.*

45

SIR WILLIAM SCHWENCK GILBERT, 1836–1911

*"The Pirates of Penzance." Autograph manuscript of the libretto (Act I only). 1879. 28 p. 26.5 x 21 cm.*

Opened to the same passage as shown in the autograph manuscript of the score.

*Purchased in 1964.*

_[The Pirates leave ~~and enter~~, mysteriously stealing... ~~distributed~~ on tiptoe, & express the flight of the girls]_

| | | |
|---|---|---|
| All | Too late! | |
| Pirates | | Ha! ha! |
| All | | Too late! |
| Pirates | | Ho! ho! |

Ha! ha! ha! ha! — Ho! ho! ho! ho!

Ensemble.

| Pirates | Ladies | Fred & Mabel |
|---|---|---|
| Now here's a prostrate opportunity | We have missed our opportunity | They have missed their opportunity |
| To get married with impunity | Of escaping with impunity | Of escaping with impunity |
| And indulge in the felicity | So farewell to the felicity | |
| Of unbounded domesticity | Of our maiden domesticity | |
| ~~You shall quickly be~~ | They shall quickly be parson-ified — | |
| ~~But are gentlemen~~ personified | | |
| Conjugally | | |
| ~~And will all be~~ matrimonified | Conjugally matrimonified — | |
| By a Doctor of Divinity | By a Doctor of Divinity | |
| ~~Who resides~~ in this vicinity! | Who resides in this vicinity! | |
| Who resides | | |

~~The pirates sing the ladies~~

Mabel, ~~coming forward~~ (recit) Hold, monsters! Ere your pirate caravanserai

Proceeds against our will to wed us all

Just bear in mind that we are wards in Chancery,

And father is a Major General!

Pirates (cowed)

~~Pirates come to the front.~~

All the ladies    We'd better pause, or dangers may befall —

Their father is a Major General!

~~All~~    Yes yes, he is a major General!

~~A major General~~

The Major General has entered unnoticed ~~at back~~ on rock

General.    ~~He~~ Yes — I am a Major General!

46

ROBERT BROWNING, 1812–1889

*"Asolando: Fancies and Facts." Autograph manuscript signed. 1889. 100 p.*
*25.5 x 19 cm.*

*Asolando* was published on the day of Browning's death in Venice on 12 December 1889. The manuscript includes thirty poems, and has been described as "a collection of love lyrics, versified anecdotes, and philosophical pronouncements." The "Epilogue," reproduced here, in which Browning describes himself, is perhaps the most familiar of the poems in the collection.

*Gift of Mr. J. P. Morgan, 1924.*

# Epilogue.

At the midnight in the silence of the sleep-time,
    When you set your fancies free,
Will they pass to where — by death, ~~you~~ <sup>boots</sup> think, imprisoned —
Low he lies who once so loved you, whom you loved so,
    — Pity me?


Oh to love so, (so) be loved, yet so mistaken!          tr
    What had I on earth to do
With the slothful, ~~and~~ <sup>with</sup> the mawkish, ~~the~~ unmanly?
Like the aimless, helpless, hopeless, did I drivel
    — Being — who?


One who never turned his back but <sup>marched</sup> ~~~~ breast forward,      p.157
    Never doubted clouds would break,
Never dreamed, though right were worsted, wrong would triumph,
Held we fall to rise, are baffled to fight better,
    Sleep to wake.


No, at noonday in the bustle of man's work-time
    Greet the unseen with a cheer!
Bid him forward, breast and back as either should be,
"Strive and thrive!" cry ~~~~ "Speed, — fight <sup>on, fare</sup> ever
    There as here!"

47

W. SOMERSET MAUGHAM, 1874–1965

*"Ah King; six stories of Malaya." Autograph manuscript signed. 1933.*
*409 leaves. 25.5 x 19.5 cm.*

On 23 October 1950 Mr. Maugham gave not only an entertaining and informative talk to the Fellows of the Library, but the manuscript of *Ah King* as well. This collection, published in 1933, contains some of his most enduring short stories, written with that straightforward clarity that is characteristic of his style. It all seems simple, until you inspect the manuscript and see the words and incidents that Mr. Maugham has changed, rearranged, or discarded. Then the labor required, even of an old hand, becomes apparent, and the mysterious process of literary creation stands documented, but not revealed. It seems appropriate to reproduce the first page of his story "The Book-bag." Reproduced with the permission of the literary executor of the Estate of W. Somerset Maugham.

*Gift of Mr. W. Somerset Maugham, 1950.*

The Book-bag.

Some people read for instruction, which is ~~praiseworthy~~ **laudable**, + some ~~people read~~ for pleasure, which is innocent, but not a few read from ~~habit~~ *depravity, vice*, & I suppose this is neither innocent nor praiseworthy. Of this lamentable band am I. Conversation after a time ~~fatigues~~ *bores* me, games ~~tire~~ me & my own thoughts, which as an author should be the unfailing resource of a sensible man, ~~I have a tendency to~~ **I have a tendency to** run dry. ~~They have a tendency I can only be quite certain that they will swarm upon me whenever my attention should be fixed upon some particular object such as listening to a concert of Brahms or hitting a golf-ball.~~ Now I fly to my book as the opium smoker to his pipe. I would sooner read the catalogue of the Army & Navy Stores or Bradshaw's guide than nothing at all, + indeed I have spent many delightful hours over both these works. At one time I never went out without a second-hand bookseller's list in my pocket. I know no reading that is more fruity. Of course to read in this way is as reprehensible as drug-taking, & I never cease to wonder at the impertinence of great readers who, because they are such, look

48

THOMAS STEARNS ELIOT, 1888–1965

*"Defence of the Islands." Autograph draft of the poem in pencil, signed in ink. 1940. 1 p. 24.5 x 20.5 cm.*

First printed as a broadside in 1940, this poem was later printed in *Britain at War*, published by the Museum of Modern Art in 1941. The manuscript is inscribed to Mrs. Marion V. Dorn, wife of the artist E. McKnight Kauffer, at whose home Eliot was staying when he wrote the poem. Autograph manuscript drafts of poems by Eliot are most uncommon. This facsimile is published with the permission of the copyright owners, Mrs. T. S. Eliot and Faber & Faber, Ltd.

*Gift of Mrs. Marion V. Dorn, 1963.*

Let these memorials of built stone, music's
grey tuneless instrument, of the generations
cultivation of the earth, of English verse

those of
Be joined in memory with the defence
of this Island ~~by those who deiden ther~~

no
And by ~~those~~ who were appointed to the
grey ships, ~~the battle cruiser~~, destroyer,
battle ship, merchant seaman, trawler,
contributing to the centuries store of
British bone on the sea floor,

us
And by ~~those~~ who, in the worlds ~~most~~
newest gamble with death, fought the
power of darkness in fire and air

our
And ~~those from century to century~~ like ~~those~~ forbears destined
to release some of their number to rest
in Flanders & in France, unchanged in
everything but their weapons

by us
And ~~those~~ again for whom the faces of
honour ~~are~~ the field ~~and streets~~ of our
~~at~~ homes —

our              generations of past and future,
Let they tell ~~to our flesh~~ and ~~four~~ kin,
and ~~they~~ who speak ~~our~~ speech,
that we

Let these memorials say to the generations
of past & future that for their sake
we took up our positions, in obedience to orders.

for Marion Dorn
in remembrance of
June 7-10, 1940 —    T. S. Eliot

49

ANTOINE DE SAINT-EXUPÉRY, 1900–1944

*"Le Petit Prince." Autograph manuscript with illustrations by the author.*
*[c.1943]. 172 p. 28 x 22 cm.*

*The Little Prince* has become a classic in the thirty years since its publication. The story, which has been called a parable for adults told as a children's story, concerns an airman forced down in the desert with a short supply of water, struggling against odds to repair the engine of his plane (as happened to Saint-Exupéry in the Sahara in 1938). The pilot tells the story of the Prince who left his asteroid, flew down to earth, and gave up his life to save his soul. The manuscript is in pencil, in a tiny hand, and is illustrated with drawings by the author—sometimes quite rudimentary in character, but always charming and meaningful.

*Purchased for the Elisabeth Ball Collection, 1968.*

Quand j'avais six ans j'ai vu une fois une magnifique image. C'était un serpent boa qui avalait un fauve. C'était à peu près comme ça.

Mais je ne savais pas dessiner ~~les~~ j'avais six ans, j'ai une fois essayé ça. C'était mon premier dessin.

Et j'ai dit aux grandes personnes : qu'est-ce que c'est ?

Elles m'ont répondu c'est un chapeau.

Ce n'était pas un chapeau. C'était un serpent boa qui digérait un éléphant. Le ~~boa~~ serpent boa avale sa proie tout entier sans la mâcher. Et il ~~doit dormir~~ . Il fait ~~alors~~ pendant ~~peu au~~ . Au bout de six mois le serpent boa est ~~devenu~~ quelle.

J'ai fait un dessin pour expliquer ça.

~~J'ai expliqué~~ aux grandes personnes ~~et pour que~~ comprennent ~~qu~~ c'était un ~~serpent~~ dessin. J'ai dessiné

l'intérieur du serpent boa.
C'était mon second dessin.

On m'a ~~conseillé~~ de laisser de côté les ~~serpents boa~~ plutôt l'histoire ~~celui et le~~ grammaire ~~et la peinture~~ et l'apprendre la ~~géographie~~ . J'ai appris ~~la géographie~~ ~~et je~~ ne ~~sais~~ plus j'aurais dessiner avec bonheur et ~~mauvaise humeur~~ et si j'ai ~~plus~~ jamais fait de ~~dessin~~ . Les grandes personnes demandent trop d'explication. ~~c'est par les temps~~ . ~~C'est~~ ~~fatiguant~~ . C'est fatiguant pour les enfants de toujours et toujours ~~donner~~ leur explication.

50

JOHN STEINBECK, 1902–1968

*"Travels with Charley." Autograph manuscript. 1961. 269 p. 30 x 20.5 cm.*

In 1962, the year in which he was awarded the Nobel Prize for Literature, John Steinbeck presented to the Library the manuscript of *Travels with Charley in Search of America*. It is entirely autograph and written on yellow pad paper, some loose ledger leaves, and in a bound ledger. Charley the French poodle accompanied Steinbeck on a rambling journey across the United States and back in a pick-up truck called Rocinante. Steinbeck's acute observations on the American scene were characterized by the Swedish Academy as "his great feeling for nature, for the tilled soil, the wasteland, the mountains and the ocean coasts." Steinbeck also presented other manuscripts and papers to the Library including the manuscript of *The Winter of Our Discontent*. Reproduced with the permission of Mrs. John Steinbeck.

*Gift of Mr. John Steinbeck, 1962.*

1.

When I was very young and the urge to be some place else was on me, I was assured by mature people that maturity would cure this itch. Still having it when years described me as mature the prescribed remedy was middle age. In middle age I was assured that greater age would calm my fever and now at fifty eight perhaps senility will do the job. Nothing has worked. Four hoarse blasts of a ships' whistle still raises the hair on my neck and sets my feet to tapping. The sound of a jet, an engine warming up, even the clopping of shod hooves on pavement brings on the ancient shudder, the dry mouth and vacant eye, the hot palms and the churn of stomach high up under the rib cage. In other words, I don't improve, in further words, once a bum always a bum. I fear the disease is incurable. I set this matter down, not to instruct others but to inform myself.

In a long and wandery life, some verities have forced themselves on me. Perhaps those among my readers who bear vagrant blood will find likeness of experience in a few generalities.

When the virus of restlessness begins to take possession of a wayward man, and the the road away from Here seems broad and straight and sweet, the victim must first find in himself a good and sufficient reason for going. This to the practical bum is not difficult. He has a built in garden of reasons to choose from. Next he must plan his trip in

# INDEX

PRODUCED BY

THE STINEHOUR PRESS

AND

THE MERIDEN GRAVURE COMPANY

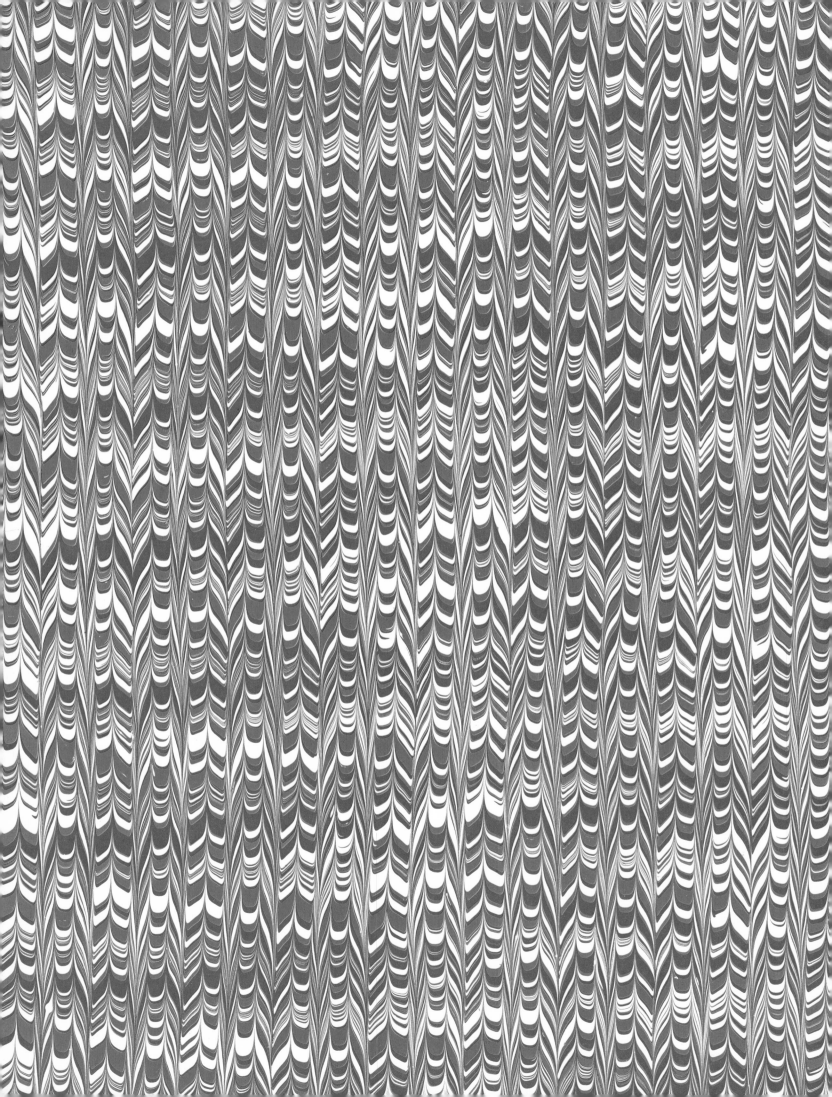